The love of money, the apostle Paul observed, is the root of evil. But properly invested and compassionately managed, money can foster much that is good. In this book, Rob Martin simply, practically, and clearly explains how this can and should be done. Replet[...] several decades of experience in the world of compassion[...] nual seminars on the subject to the culturally eclectic resi[...] in New Haven and is uniquely accessible to Christian lea[...] mend this book.

JON BONK, J & J Bonk, author of *Missions and Money: Aff*[...]

In my African context, reading *When Money Goes on Mission* is like having the privilege of being seated under the village tree with a wise elder and being nourished by the transformative spring of wisdom coming from his lifelong experience in mission. The amazing and sobering stories, the deep biblical and theological insights on stewardship, the simplicity and the beauty of Rob's writing elevated my spirit. The book deeply shifted my paradigm and transformed my understanding of biblical fundraising. I found this a most useful and relevant book on fundraising that connects with my majority world context. The benefit will be immense for everyone who reads it, especially for mission and church leaders from the majority word.

DANIEL BOURDANNÉ, General Secretary, IFES

I have served on the board of First Fruit for many years and have observed Rob's imparting these principles to both ministries and granting organizations. I have seen the importance of this message and this "methodology" of bridging the "money gap" in which both ministries and donors must grapple. Rob not only offers proven answers, but also gives us paths to true sustainability as organizations see that money is not the real issue. Leadership and a realignment with true biblical principles are what is often needed, and Rob shows us how.

HENRY CLOUD, author and leadership consultant

Having worked and traveled with Rob Martin for nearly thirty years, I have come to respect and admire his penetrating insights about money and missions, and his ability to cut through promotional fog and to see clearly what truly effective ministry looks like. This book distills the best of Rob's wisdom, interlaced with profound biblical insight and sprinkled with lively humor. I recommend it as a "must read" for anyone who is giving or raising money.

DAVID W. BENNETT, Global Associate Director for Collaboration and Content, Lausanne Movement Board Member, First Fruit, Inc.

Rob Martin masterfully tells stories to communicate a powerful message about the communion of giving and receiving. You will find yourself laughing, nodding in agreement, then best of all, you will discover that on the adventure, like a wise, old friend, he helped you learn how to rally local sustainable support, how to earn trust with excellence and keep it with accountability, and how to encourage financial transactions in a way that fosters spiritual transformation. If you are engaged in God's global mission, read this book to lift your learning curve heavenward.

GARY G. HOAG, ECFA International Liaison

Rob Martin's brilliance as both a mission's director and a global funder of evangelical ministry is on full display in this highly practical and story-based narrative of co laborative funding principles and practices. Everyone on the journey of *money on mission*—local or global donors, ministry leaders or workers, board members or executives—would benefit from implementing what they learn from Rob's experience in mobilizing more resources to catalyze and sustain God's work.

RON WILLIAMS, chairman of Cornerstone Trust

The church knows that something urgently needs to change in the global economy of missions today, but what and how? In *When Money Goes on Mission*, the Lord uses fundraising sage Rob Martin to connect the dots of mission history to find "a true and equal partnership in a cross-cultural or international setting, where each offers the other what they need in pursuit of their mutual callings." Magnificently presented!

BARBARA SHANTZ, advisor, Give Way Visioneering; co-catalyst of Lausanne Ministry Fundraising Network

It is easy to give money naively, never understanding that your gift made a difficult situation worse. It is also easy to decide that it is best to never give, justified by the idea that outside funding harms people and leads to dependency. The more challenging space is to remain open to the leading of the Holy Spirit and discerning regarding the character of leaders, the viability of financial processes and ministry strategies, and the impact of cultural realities and expectations, to know how to share God's resources in God's mission in ways that truly further His purposes and foster ever-deepening growth and spiritual maturity for everyone involved. That is the focus of this book and why it is so important to read!

MARY LEDERLEITNER, author of *Cross-Cultural Partnership: Navigating the Complexities of Money and Mission*

The dean of Christian philanthropy, Rob Martin, solves the puzzle of charities asking and donors giving in *When Money Goes on Mission*. A must buy.

TOM MCCALLIE, President, Westwood Endowment Former Executive Director, The Maclellan Foundation, Inc.

Rob Martin has coached mission leaders from over forty nations and has equipped hundreds of leaders in undeveloped economies to create funding sources in their own contexts. Rob has also provided new insights and practical tools for these leaders to build sustained relationships across oceans that avoid toxic charity and create joy for both donors and mission leaders. Captured by the phrase "sustained interdependence," *When Money Goes on Mission* names a whole new way of understanding philanthropy and fundraising that will quickly become the standard to which we all aspire.

BRAD SMITH, President, Bakke Graduate University

Rob Martin has written a ground-breaking book on money and mission. A storyteller well versed with on-the-ground experience, he opens the world of donors and doers. While money for mission is complex, he links the dynamics of asking, giving, and raising funds. His vision is well expressed by when "the giver and the receiver... are in communion... [they] are equal at the foot of the cross." This rich resource will be the go-to text for years to come.

BRIAN C. STILLER, Global Ambassador, World Evangelical Alliance

Any of those fortunate enough to be in mission realize that we stand on the shoulders of the saints who have gone before us. Rob is one such person, and the lessons he shares in these pages are as thoughtful as they are engaging. This is not a book of theories and platitudes; it is a memoir of wisdom and experience that will make any reader a better disciple. If you are involved in mission, then you must read this book. Quickly!

JUSTIN NARDUCCI, President/Chief Executive Officer, Lifewater International

Rob virtually invented what became known as "field visits." Unwilling to just read proposals, Rob wanted to look petitioners in the eye and see who they really were and what they really did. People from around the world seek his counsel. Now his book brings a fresh, thoughtful, and vitally important perspective on money—giving and receiving. Humble and always with good humor, he has written this book with his life.

PHILL BUTLER, founder of InterCristo, InterDev, and Vision Synergy

Why another book on fundraising? Rob Martin's amazing insight is a fitting response to this question given how his book bridges a noticeable gap in many of the previously written materials. Rob begins with a personal story and highlights the important role that God plays in funding His work. From the very beginning, he clearly submitted that God is at the center of fundraising and support development. I commend the book to everyone and pray that you experience joy as you encounter God in your own journey in fundraising.

KEHINDE OJO, Indigenous Support Development Director, IFES

When I met Rob Martin, I was impressed with his insight into the challenges faced by my friends in Latin America who were trying desperately to find a way to pay the bills so they could build ministries from which to fulfill their calling. It was not so much his professional insight that made the difference, but his willingness to make their struggle his own. As a result, his new book is not about how money goes on mission, but a compilation of lessons he learned from his new friends as they all went on mission together. The Spirit of God is doing a new work in our day—in which new mission initiatives are emerging around the world in places that we in the West thought of as our mission field. As Rob immersed himself in this new work, he humbly learned lessons we can all use, and he wrote them down in *When Money Goes on Mission*.

TIMOTHY HALLS, Executive Coordinator, Martureo—the Brazilian Center for Missiological Reflection

When I first began leading a missions organization, I was given the (unsolicited) advice from a friend: "You need to get to know and learn from Rob Martin. He knows more about fundraising than you will ever learn." This is also my advice to you. Rob tells stories with a punch. He also is a blunt teller of truth when he needs to be. Reading his advice about writing proposals is worth the price of this book. You don't have to learn everything in the school of hard knocks and mistakes. Instead, read Rob's book.

GREG PRITCHARD, Director, European Leadership Forum President, Forum of Christian Leaders

Rob has a unique understanding of fund development and the changes that have taken place over the last few decades. His book provides a great deal of wisdom to leaders as they navigate their way forward in this area. Rob is a gift to Christian organizations, and his book is a "must read" for directors and leaders around the world.

JANET MORGAN, Scripture Union International Director (2004–2017)

As one of the original founders of The Gathering, Rob Martin—through his wisdom, encouragement, humor, spiritual maturity, and friendship—has shaped the growth of global Christian philanthropy for decades. He is a sage and a treasure.

FRED SMITH, President of The Gathering

Rob Martin never settles for easy answers or tired patterns. He teaches mission leaders and donors to blend together creative thinking, intense passion, expansive vision, and unwavering faith to guarantee the highest kingdom value from every gift.

ROGER PARROTT, President, Belhaven University

In spite of the good will and well-meaning intentions of givers—whom Rob Martin describes and honors in his book—the subtle power of the money-as-master paradigm has shaped how we think about, strategize, and prioritize our kingdom relationships. No one knows better than Rob the agonies and joys of serving the global church from the angle of financial resourcing. He knows the mission field from inside as much as any nonresident can. He has been diligent and intelligent in learning all he can from the people he serves on the field and at home. His book helps us return money back to its proper and God-honoring place in Christian mission, thinking, and practice. It captures his wealth of knowledge and experience and converts it into an essential tool to help us rethink and reshape our mission service.

ALEXANDRE ARAUJO, consultant for Partnering with Global North and South Missions Movements

Rob Martin is a prophetic voice reminding us of the sacredness of the exchange between the giver and receiver. When the granting is given and received with respect and in the right spirit, it moves beyond the transactional and becomes transformative for both the giver and receiver.

STEVE PERRY, cofounder of Sacred Harvest Foundation; author of *Living with Wealth without Losing Your Soul*

This book is full of practical and biblical wisdom about fund raising that Rob learned through years of experience as both a fund raiser and a donor. Not only will you learn a great deal as you read, but you'll also remember what you learn because Rob is a great storyteller. Those colorful stories clearly illustrate his points and are both personal as well as unforgettable.

JANE OVERSTREET, President and CEO, DAI

This is the book we have been waiting for. Rob Martin is a trustworthy and experienced voice both for Christian philanthropists and ministry leaders. Few people have been more influential in shaping generous giving in mission around the world in the last thirty years. Rob's larger-than-life persona, wisdom, senses of humor, and uncompromisingly direct style of communication come through. He has been sharing these stories and invaluable lessons for years, and now I can't wait for a new generation of Christians to hear them.

JOSÉ DE DIOS, Coordinator, International Partnering Associates (IPA)

The communion of giving and receiving is a radical paradigm in mobilizing God's resources for ministries that can change the way people think about fundraising. Rob does not just write about concepts and theories but describes how money goes to mission in ways that transform both the giver and the receiver. His own spiritual journey, juxtaposed with funding missions, shows how the communion of giving and receiving grows people to greater understanding, trust, and love toward a common vision for the Gospel.

ZENET MARAMARA, Asian Theological Seminary, Manila; Christian Stewardship Association

This book should be required reading for anyone involved in grant-making and leadership of a mission agency, as well as members of church missions boards. Rob Martin is one of the most respected and esteemed grant makers in the world, appreciated equally in the Western and Majority worlds. Fusing principles and storytelling, he traces the evolution of US grant-making in the last forty years, both in many grant-making agencies and in his own thinking. His reflections are principled, insightful, weighty, humble, helpful, and biblically rooted. Grant-makers and grant-receivers who heed and apply these principles are more likely to benefit from deeper partnerships and more God-honoring and fruitful ministries.

LINDSAY BROWN, former General Secretary, International Fellowship of Evangelical Students (IFES); former International Director, The Lausanne Movement

In this moment of great change and unprecedented opportunity for the global church, Rob Martin is a trusted and experienced guide. Far more than a "how to guide" for raising funds, this book is about how to partner for Christ's mission in ways that reflect our communion as God's people!

JOHN BERNARD, President, United World Mission

Biblical, insightful, and immensely practical, this book brings together Rob Martin's decades of expertise in leadership, fundraising, and partnership development for faith-based organizations. No stone is left unturned in helping the reader understand the process of developing outcome-based strategies that will motivate and draw partners (here and around the world) into a relationship of mutual stewardship and accountability in accomplishing the Great Commission. The principles in this book, if followed, can help change the destiny of your leadership and mission for God's glory—it changed mine!

STEVEN R. JOHNSON, Executive Vice President for Strategic Advancement, Phoenix Seminary

Rob Martin has produced a masterpiece. His book on mission and money will be an invaluable source of wisdom for pastors, mission leaders, philanthropists, and all who are entrusted with the responsibility of raising and giving money. As one who has been mentored by Rob, I am profoundly grateful to have benefitted from his strong and curious intellect, his joyful personality, the rich qualities of his faith, his depth of expertise, and his generosity of spirit. This book, like his life, is a source of wisdom, hope, and joy.

S. DOUGLAS BIRDSALL, Honorary Chair, The Lausanne Movement

WHEN MONEY GOES ON MISSION

Fundraising and Giving in the 21st Century

ROB MARTIN

MOODY PUBLISHERS

CHICAGO

All Scripture quotations, unless otherwise indicated, are taken from the Holy Bible, New International Version®, NIV®. Copyright © 1973, 1978, 1984, 2011 by Biblica, Inc.™ Used by permission of Zondervan. All rights reserved worldwide. www.zondervan.com. The "NIV" and "New International Version" are trademarks registered in the United States Patent and Trademark Office by Biblica, Inc.™

All emphasis in Scripture has been added.

Published in association with the literary agency of Yates and Yates, LLC, 1551 N. Tustin Ave., Suite 710, Santa Ana, California 92705.

Names and details of some stories have been changed to protect the privacy of individuals.

Edited by Amanda Cleary Eastep
Interior Design: Ragont Design
Cover Design: Erik M. Peterson
Cover illustration copyright © 2018 by PureSolution/Shutterstock (366850607). All rights reserved.
Author photo credit: Melissa Mersereau Sanchez

All websites and phone numbers listed herein are accurate at the time of publication but may change in the future or cease to exist. The listing of website references and resources does not imply publisher endorsement of the site's entire contents. Groups and organizations are listed for informational purposes, and listing does not imply publisher endorsement of their activities.

ISBN: 978-0-8024-1884-5

We hope you enjoy this book from Moody Publishers. Our goal is to provide high-quality, thought-provoking books and products that connect truth to your real needs and challenges. For more information on other books and products written and produced from a biblical perspective, go to www.moodypublishers.com or write to:

Moody Publishers
820 N. LaSalle Boulevard
Chicago, IL 60610

1 3 5 7 9 10 8 6 4 2

Printed in the United States of America

For Peter and Gail Ochs
Thanks for sharing the peaches

CONTENTS

FOREWORD

I FIRST MET ROB MARTIN in 1998. The previous year I had left my position as an assistant professor at a major research university to join the faculty of Covenant College, a small, Christian liberal arts college in Lookout Mountain, Georgia. I was hoping to start an academic program and a training center that would address poverty from a distinctively Christian perspective. I barely knew what I was talking about, and I certainly wasn't qualified to be launching a new organization.

As I was struggling to put the pieces together, I was invited to attend a small conference hosted by First Fruit, the Christian foundation where Rob served as Executive Director for many years. During one of the lunch breaks, Rob asked me to go for a walk with him. He inquired about my vision, goals, and plans, and I fumbled around trying to come up with some coherent thoughts. At one point I said, "My biggest concern is that I hate even the thought of fundraising, and I hope I never have to do it." Rob's warm and jovial demeanor suddenly changed. Looking upset, he asked, "And how do you think that makes me feel?"

I was deeply embarrassed. I was a rookie at all of this, but even I could sense that I had crossed some line in this strange new world of philanthropy. My mind started racing with questions: *Why was Rob so offended? Why was he taking this so personally? Why would he care if I didn't want to beg people to give me money?*

As Rob mentored me over the subsequent two decades, I slowly began to understand the answers to those questions.

I realized that I had been thinking of fundraising as a necessary evil, as the pain that organizations had to endure to achieve their mission. And it was a pain that I wanted to avoid at all costs. Like many other nonprofit leaders, I believed that donors should just "pay, pray, and get out of the way" so that we experts could get on with *our* work.

In contrast, for Rob the act of giving and receiving funds is a deeply spiritual activity, a sacred communion whose significance is of far greater importance than the dollars being transacted. And Rob is right. When both the givers and receivers of funds bring their respective gifts into a mutually respectful partnership, they reflect who they really are together: the very embodiment of Jesus Christ in this broken and hurting world (1 Corinthians 12). When money goes on mission, the triune God goes on mission.

Rob was right to be offended by my disdain for fundraising, for God Himself was offended.

Through the years, First Fruit and other donors demonstrated through their words and actions what a communion of giving and receiving entailed, discipling me and standing with me through many ups and downs. And the results have been dramatic. Despite its many warts, the Chalmers Center, the training center I started at Covenant College, has been used by God to equip churches through a variety of training resources, including the bestselling book *When Helping Hurts: How to Alleviate Poverty without Hurting the Poor . . . and Yourself.* When money goes on mission, rookies get both forgiveness and mentoring. And through this restored communion, God's kingdom miraculously grows.

Indeed, the kingdom is advancing dramatically through the exploding church in the majority world of Africa, Asia, and Latin America. As historian Philip Jenkins notes in his book *The Next Christendom: The Coming of Global Christianity*, the typical Christian in the twenty-first century is not a businessperson attending a megachurch in an American suburb but rather a poor woman in a slum in São Paulo, Brazil or a poor man in a village in Nigeria. How can Western Christians, who are the richest people ever to walk the face of the earth, use our vast resources, power, and technology to support the ministries of our brothers and sisters in the majority world?

For Rob, the foundation of our approach in the majority world is not built on our money, power, or technology. Rather, it is built on the same foundation that he established with me: the deep communion that emerges when the giver and the receiver of funds bow together at the foot of the cross. For as they do so, the money does more than change hands; it goes on mission, God's mission.

Rob has been involved in various aspects of philanthropy for forty years, traveling to seventy countries to support ministries on the very frontiers of Christ's ever-expanding kingdom. Drawing on this lifetime of experience, Rob shares both his mind and heart in this profoundly timely book. May these pages impact your life as deeply as Rob has impacted mine.

BRIAN FIKKERT
President of the Chalmers Center at Covenant College
Coauthor of *When Helping Hurts* and *Becoming Whole*

INTRODUCTION

FORTY YEARS AGO, on what passes for a miserable winter night in Southern California, I was unexpectedly recruited into the "family business" of God and His children.

A few weeks earlier, I'd become a Christian when I was swept up in the Jesus People revival at Calvary Chapel, a church in Costa Mesa, California, that was in the midst of a phenomenal time of growth. I was thirty-three—older than most who were finding Christ there at the time. Becoming a follower of Jesus was a revelation for me and quite literally an experience of going from death to life. I felt like I was recovering in the hospital following a train wreck and would be getting a new start on life. And I wanted to learn all about it.

Fortunately, Calvary Chapel had things going on around the clock, and I took in all I could, attending a different Bible study every day. I even attended women's studies while quietly sitting in the back of the sanctuary. I began seeing life from a whole new perspective, and my spirit came alive.

Other Calvary Chapel Bible studies were being conducted off campus, and one in particular had drawn my attention. It was advertised for writers, artists, photographers, and journalists. I was trained as a newspaperman and had a middling career working in just about all the facets of editorial, including photography, newswriting, and even a stint as a sports editor. I went to this particular study because working again in newspapers was the one thing in my pre-Christian existence that I desperately wanted to return to. I hoped somebody at the Bible study might make the right connections for me.

Somebody did, and it set me in the right direction.

When the study group's leader learned of my background and realized I was the only person there who'd actually scratched out a living writing and taking pictures, he asked me to fulfill a photography need he knew about. The Orange County Rescue Mission was applying for a community service award given annually by Disneyland to deserving local nonprofits, and pictures of their work were required.

The Mission, known as the Rescue "Center" back then, was located in a seedy part of Santa Ana near the bus terminal. When I arrived there in the chilly January mist, I saw about a hundred people or so standing along the sidewalk. They were waiting, as I would soon learn, for the nightly meal and evangelistic service to begin. These folks struck me as the sort of people that others would quietly slide to the opposite side of the street to avoid. I waded into the middle of the crowd, putting on my practiced look of reporter confidence that said, "I'm here on serious business." The crowd parted slightly, and I found myself in a dingy foyer lit by a 60-watt light bulb hanging at the end of a wire.

The foyer led to a small auditorium crammed with rickety metal chairs in various hues of rust and chipped paint. Up front was a platform with a small wooden pulpit and a battered upright piano. The room's side walls were painted with lurid murals depicting the terrors of hell and wonders of heaven. Also pictured were narrow bridges connecting the terrors and the wonders; on these bridges, wayfarers walked into the light from the darkness behind, though some were falling off the bridge into a chasm of flames licking upward.

Beyond the auditorium, through a single door, was a make-shift dining room with a modest kitchen in one corner, exuding the smell of burbling stew. Lining the dining room walls were fifteen or so refrigerators, all in the throes of death to judge by the cacophony of metal-on-metal shrieks emanating from their compressors. A spider web of extension cords connected these fridges to a few overcrowded electric outlets.

Upstairs I found the Mission's sleeping quarters—a small room with threadbare carpet overlaid on worn linoleum, and with so many bunkbeds crammed in, I was sure no fire inspector had ever seen it. The rat traps strewn under the bunks and the overwhelming odor of too many men who'd taken too few show-ers convinced me that a health inspector hadn't been there either.

I took what pictures I could and thought, though the photos were dramatic, *These can't be helpful.*

The service in the auditorium began, and I made my way downstairs into a scene only Jesus could love. The crowd over-flowed into the foyer and out to the street. On the platform, a preacher was on his knees imploring his listeners not to live as he had. He described himself as being "so low, I once cold-cocked my mother because she told me she loved me." Staring back at him with expressions of disgust or disinterest—it was hard to tell which—were homeless men and women of the streets, the people no one wanted: broken Vietnam War veterans, bag ladies, alcoholics, panhandlers, the mentally ill, grifters and drifters. To the Mission staff, they were collectively known as "the least, the last, and the lost."

I took more photos, focusing in on faces and profiles in the crowd as they sat through the service and put something—only God knew what—into the offering plate. Later, after the "ear banging" (their term for the worship service), they ate their meal and found out if they would be one of the lucky ones to get a bed for the night.

My assignment done, I put away my camera and tried to make a fast exit into the fresh air outside. As I was elbowing my way through the throng and had the street in sight, a large hand grasped my right shoulder and propelled me through a different door. I stood in the office of the Mission's founder, the Reverend Lewis Whitehead, a six-foot-three, three-hundred-pound African American and former Marine sergeant. Lewis's eyes bored holes into mine. "Son," he began, "the Lord has need of you."

His hand guided me to a chair in front of his desk. As he rounded the desk to his seat, he asked, "What are you doing right now?"

I didn't think lying was a good idea. "Nothing," I answered.

A warm smile came across his face. "Would you make a slide presentation and prepare some thoughts for me to take around to churches to promote the Mission?"

"Sure," I said, for reasons I couldn't fathom at the time.

Although I didn't know it, I had just accepted an "internship" with the "family business" of God and His children.

The next morning, with nothing else useful to do, I showed up uncharacteristically early to my unpaid position and began ratcheting through 35-mm film documenting the Mission's neighborhood, which was the underbelly of a fabulously rich corner of the United States.

In the first few minutes on the job, I startled a somnolent derelict who snapped awake, waved a gun at me, and shouted something incomprehensible, which I took to mean, "Get out!" As much as I wanted to comply, I froze in my tracks like a possum and blurted out, "Jesus loves you!"

I don't recommend this as an evangelistic strategy, and I don't believe it was effective in this particular circumstance. In fact, I wasn't really trying to save his soul. I think somewhere in my primordial subconscious, my brain was trying to use God as an amulet to stop any bullet headed my way.

Clearly unimpressed, and probably only slightly more lost than I, the man dismissively waved me off and slipped back into his stupor.

Thus began my career in missions.

Later that afternoon, I learned my first real and most important fundraising lesson. I'd stationed myself in the Mission's dining area to take photos of the staff preparing the nightly meal. They were all recently saved souls whom Lewis had plucked from the proverbial "gutter"—or, as it was more gently referred to, "the highways and byways." No photograph of mine could capture how noisy and dingy this room was. But it was, for all its faded glory, the heart of the Mission's feeding program. As I entered, I discovered the staff was methodically going from one ice-chocked fridge to another, discovering there was no meat or even vegetables for them to prepare for the stew pot that night.

Undaunted, and certainly not frantic, they gathered to pray and pulled me into their circle of arm-pumping petitions to God for food to feed the hungry and homeless that night. This put me on alert that I'd wandered into an alternate universe of some sort. Don't you go to the store when you need food? I'd heard about praying for stuff, but not stuff you *needed*—that stuff you bought. What you prayed for was stuff you *wanted*, like a new bike—which, I think, besides the sinner's prayer I'd squeaked out just a few weeks before, was the last "thing" I'd ever prayed for. And even that I ended up buying when I was a kid with my paper route earnings. In any case, there we were praying—that is, *they* were praying; I was holding on for dear life—when a loud, insistent knocking at the front door interrupted us. It kept up until the prayer couldn't go on.

A few of us broke away and opened the door to discover a short, balding man in a loud sports coat, pointing with a dead stogie in his hand to the biggest Cadillac I'd ever seen. He asked, "Could you guys use some steak for dinner?" He turned out to be a frozen food broker heading home from a convention with a trunkful of samples that were defrosting. Not wanting to see them wasted, he'd found our address in the phone book.

This scene scrambled my brain.

The staff wasn't surprised. They'd prayed; the food showed up. What else was there to say?

I'd just witnessed a miracle, an in-breaking of God. It was one of my first "Ebenezers," basically, a moment marked as such with a stone of remembrance (see 1 Sam. 7:12). God's love for the weakest among us is breathtaking. All we have to do is want to help. My lessons had begun.

Volunteering at the Mission didn't pay my bills. However, thankfully, after a few weeks there I received the first money I'd earned in a long time—six hundred dollars from a temporary job. As I went to cash the check, the idea to give a tithe tugged at my mind. This thought ushered me into a slithering selfish mood. I didn't want to give any of it away.

I walked awhile on the streets of Santa Ana that morning trying to figure out what was driving this conflict. Then it hit me. I was struggling with my belief in God. Why would I give sixty dollars or even sixty cents to something that was a fantasy? This new life I was living, this new view of the world I was learning, this healing of my soul I was experiencing—was it all real, or an illusion?

I don't know whether recalling the incident with the frozen food broker tipped the scales or not, but I do know I decided that day to recognize the truth about God. Not only was He *not* an illusion, He was the deepest reality of my life.

I then joyfully gave away a portion of those first funds and sensed that I'd become a true disciple, a follower of Jesus. I didn't yet fully understand that I had given something precious for something much greater. I had just experienced the unadulterated joy of giving.

The primary lessons that emerged from these obscure beginnings help inform this book. In the succeeding years, I have done fundraising and philanthropy for mission; I have led mission and been led in mission. I have been managed by and have been privileged to manage some of the finest servants in the family business. More importantly, for the ideas imparted here, I have traveled to seventy countries and have observed up close the heroic work of missions as the light has penetrated into some of the most trying places on earth. These observations have led to what some might call pattern recognition. Well, I would hope so! In twenty-five of those years, I read countless proposals with strategies from missional entrepreneurs and from missions—large, small, Western and non-Western. I read proposals drawn from every field of endeavor imaginable, written by artists, businesspeople, and all sorts of Christ followers, who, like Lewis but in their own unique callings, have been seeking to roll back the darkness wherever they have encountered it.

Though at first, like Jonah, I didn't want the path God had shown me to take, no matter what other life path I could've taken—or even imagined—nothing could ever come close to this journey that I so reluctantly began. And mine, like yours, is just one of millions of stories of God's redemptive ways.

So why this book?

Lewis fired up my imagination of what God wants to do when we say yes to His urgings. One of his favorite parables is found in Luke chapter 14. It is a parable of Jesus inviting the gentiles to join the Jews in communion. Lewis took the implication of the story to mean that the people most reviled in society are the very people Jesus refers to when He says if we serve them, we serve Him.

> **THOUGH AT FIRST, LIKE JONAH, I DIDN'T WANT TO TAKE THE PATH GOD HAD SHOWN ME, NO OTHER PATH I COULD HAVE TAKEN—OR EVEN IMAGINED—COULD COME CLOSE TO THIS JOURNEY.**

Then Jesus said to his host, "When you give a luncheon or a dinner, do not invite your friends, your brothers or sisters, your relatives, or your rich neighbors; if you do, they may invite you back and so you will be repaid. But when you give a banquet, invite the poor, the crippled, the lame, the blind, and you will be blessed. Although they cannot repay you, you will be repaid at the resurrection of the righteous."

When one of those at the table with him heard this, he said to Jesus, "Blessed is the one who will eat at the feast in the kingdom of God."

Jesus replied: "A certain man was preparing a great banquet and invited many guests. At the time of the banquet he sent his servant to tell those who had been invited, 'Come, for everything is now ready.'

But they all alike began to make excuses. The first said, 'I have just bought a field, and I must go and see it. Please excuse me.'

Another said, 'I have just bought five yoke of oxen, and I'm on my way to try them out. Please excuse me.'

Still another said, 'I just got married, so I can't come.'

The servant came back and reported this to his master. Then the owner of the house became angry and ordered his servant, 'Go out quickly into the streets and alleys of the town and bring in the poor, the crippled, the blind and the lame.'

'Sir,' the servant said, 'what you ordered has been done, but there is still room.'

Then the master told his servant, 'Go out to the roads and country lanes and compel them to come in, so that my house will be full. I tell you, not one of those who were invited will get a taste of my banquet.'" (Luke 14:12–24)

This was how I was introduced to missions. The staff of the Rescue Mission walked the streets of our town inviting the homeless to find hope, or at least a warm meal and a bed.

The banquet guest who inspired the parable with His words, "Blessed is the one who will eat at the feast in the kingdom of God" was foreshadowing the marriage supper of the Lamb, found in Revelation chapter 19. It is one of my favorite Scriptures, for it is the work of mission.

> Then I heard what sounded like a great multitude, like the roar of rushing waters and like loud peals of thunder, shouting:
> "Hallelujah!
> For our Lord God Almighty reigns.
> Let us rejoice and be glad
> and give him glory!
> For the wedding of the Lamb has come,
> and his bride has made herself ready.
> Fine linen, bright and clean,
> was given her to wear."

(Fine linen stands for the righteous acts of God's holy people.)

> Then the angel said to me, "Write this: Blessed are those who are invited to the wedding supper of the Lamb!" And he added, "These are the true words of God." (Rev. 19:6–9)

> He who testifies to these things says, "Yes, I am coming soon."
> Amen. Come, Lord Jesus. (Rev. 22:20)

Here in the closing pages of Revelation, we find a most beautiful and unexpected picture; the good deeds of God's children are like threads in the wedding dress of the bride, a garment worn at the marriage banquet of the Lamb. Every time we carry out a loving action of the gospel or each time the organization we are part of encourages a loving action of the gospel, it is like a thread is sewn into the bride's gown in preparation for this banquet. The purpose of missions is to prepare the bride for this wondrous marriage banquet when the Lord will drink of the vine again. It's about the joy of feasting with the least, the last, and the lost (among whom I once was)—those who, at one time, never knew such a life, represented by the banquet, ever existed . . . let alone that they would be invited.

Like the apostles and saints who came before us, we can joyfully anticipate the fruit of our work. It's our joyful task as we reach out in loving actions—to send messengers, disciple, give, pray, and witness to the truth that overcomes evil.

At First Fruit, a grant-making foundation where I've served since 1990, we hope family foundation resources will help the leaders and organizations that work among the poorest segments of the "majority world" so that we all can flourish in our mutual calling to invite the least, the last, and the lost to the banquet table.

It is my hope that if you share in this love of God's work, whether as a giver to missions or as a receiver supported by the resources of others expressing their love for God through you, this book will help you navigate the course God has shown you, and you will find a true communion of giving and receiving in what may be the greatest expansion of Christianity since the earliest days of our faith.

Let's begin the adventure.

Part One

COMMUNING: SURFING THE WAVE OF TWENTY-FIRST CENTURY MISSION

THE COMMUNION OF GIVING AND RECEIVING

WHEN MONEY "goes on mission," it travels in the form of financial gifts, carried along in the pockets of those who spend it on the ordinary things of life and ministry, so they can do the extraordinary things God has called them to do. What follows is a story of one of these extraordinary things. It is a real-life parable about an American, a Romanian, an Egyptian, and an old pair of gym socks.

Daniel[1] was a young man on the rise when he became the children's pastor of a church in California. What he didn't know was that his position would eventually lead him to accept God's call to become a paradigm buster in Poland as the country emerged from the shadow of Soviet domination. Daniel is an explorer, a man full of faith and curiosity. His questions often lead him into uncharted territory; and occasionally, his prodding introduces him to useful, paradigm-shifting ideas.

In Poland, he landed on a big one. He realized the Polish church leaders he was working with to establish an early childhood Christian education program were not only his heroes for how they had endured and even flourished under the iron grip of communism, they were as capable as he was to lead the national mission he had founded. What they needed was for Daniel to show them how to run the ministry and to help them take full ownership.

They decided they would divide responsibilities. Daniel would manage the ministry until it reached its potential, and he would raise the money back home to help the Polish leaders develop and expand the work as it grew. This created a problem. The work grew—and outgrew Daniel's ability to raise sufficient funds.

The pressure ramped up when a Romanian leader asked Daniel to help him establish a similar work in his country. Daniel scratched up the funds to help the Romanian leader start up the ministry following the same model they used in Poland. It wasn't long before church leaders from other countries requested Daniel to help them as well. It was hard and slow work to expand into a new country. The launch of each new ministry required establishing a publishing house for their materials, setting up training programs for educators, and creating demanding communication and marketing strategies. Besides the hard work, it also took a lot of money.

To finance the work, Daniel traveled back and forth to California, where he, his key supporters, and board members organized a series of fundraising events, including successful charity golf tournaments and blind auctions.

The joint events featured sponsorships from local businesses and friends of the ministry who provided generous donations—excursions, stays in vacation villas, home decorating items, spa treatments, objects of art, and even a luxury automobile if someone could sink a hole in one. This raised a lot of money, but the ministries in Europe continued to grow and outpaced even these new funding initiatives.

The blind auctions, however, set Daniel and the ministry on a whole new unintended path of fundraising. The impact of the success of his fundraising ideas raised a question in Daniel's mind. How could he grow the work in Christ's way, since Christ Himself had seemingly blessed the ministries in Europe? He sought a better way, just as he had when he gave authority of the work in Poland to the leaders he had mentored.

He did not go down the natural path of most Western fundraisers, doing more fundraising himself. After prayer and seeking counsel, Daniel decided to go down the "radical" path of encouraging the Romanian and Polish leaders to raise money in their own settings. They already had taken responsibility for the work in their countries. Now they needed to complete the transition and take responsibility for their own fundraising.

Then Daniel had a new idea. He began to only offer challenge grants; that is, matching funds. For every dollar he raised for them, he wanted these leaders to raise a dollar locally.

Daniel feared creating a paternalistic over dog/underdog approach in this new funding relationship, and, despite their raw recruit status, Daniel always treated his partner ministry leaders as equals. His job was just to show them how he did it. He invited the leader of the Romanian expansion to attend one of the golf tournaments and blind auction fundraisers in California.

The leader completely embraced the idea of taking over fundraising efforts, and to Daniel's surprise, he decided to set up his own blind auction in Romania to see if it would prime the pump of local giving. Just like Daniel, the leader went to his friends in the local churches and asked them to donate items for their first ever blind auction.

A dear soul in the community enthusiastically gave all he could, literally—an old pair of gym socks, washed, folded neatly, and priced at two leu, or fifty cents. With this widow's-mite gift, he sparked a revolution.

Before long, the idea of local funding for early childhood education ministry was embraced wholeheartedly by the Romanian Christian community. In short order, within the Romanian context, they were raising significant amounts of money in a manner that had not been done before. And though independent, they still were in deep covenant fellowship with Daniel and other national ministries that were emerging. Each of these ministries was facing a similar challenge to take responsibility for their own governance and funding while still maintaining that same fellowship with Daniel. They entered into a relationship that was not hierarchical but was simply a community of trust and accountability to a set of values, principles, and a mutual purpose.

Next, the Romanian leader, though only barely able to cover the core expenses of his own work, decided he would do for someone else what Daniel had done for him. That is, he would join in the joy of helping the global expansion of the ministry by sending encouragement in the form of a financial love gift to an Egyptian leader who, like he had been a few years earlier, was beginning to plant a new work in Egypt.

Daniel shifted focus from himself and what he could do to a focus on the mission and what these indigenous leaders could achieve independently, and in doing so, birthed a new paradigm out of the old, unlocking the local resources of the Poles, Romanians, and Egyptians.

In general, money passing from one person to another is a transaction, nothing more than an exchange of something of value for something of value in return. However, unlike everyday financial transactions, when ministries fundraise and Christians give for the mission of sharing Christ, the true value is eternal, not temporal. The gift is given to encourage a transformative act, a loving action of the gospel, where good gets down to work at the very furthest extension of mission, darkness is penetrated, and those around the world created in His image are delivered from deprivation, injustice, loneliness, and the grip of Satan.

WHEN MONEY GOES ON MISSION, IT CREATES A COMMUNION OF GIVING AND RECEIVING.

At its best, when money goes on mission, it not only supports the transformative work among those being served, it also creates a communion of giving and receiving among givers, mission leadership, and "missional entrepreneurs" from around the world—just as Daniel, the ministry leaders from Poland and Romania, and their international and local donors experienced. Though the Lord is always faithful, this communion is fragile, fraught as much with potential misunderstanding as it is bright with promise. In the past few decades, Western givers and receivers have faced significant changes regarding the getting, giving, and accounting for money in missions as the predictable world of mission finance became disrupted by the explosive growth of the church in the majority, non-Western, world.

This swell of majority-world Christians and the missional entrepreneurs among them need to acquire the funding and gain the organizational skills to assume full—and equal—partnership with their non-indigenous brother and sister missions. They need funders and mission leaders—both in the West and locally—to partner with them, to support their desire to take responsibility for their ministries, and to help them establish best biblical practices within their own contexts. This shift—away from the way mission funding had been carried out over the past two hundred years—involves the encouragement of local funding and leadership development. This new paradigm of mission finance brings the whole of the missions community and those interested in knowing more about successful mission into alignment with what God is doing today.

Also, in this new paradigm, givers in partnership with ministries want to be more involved in their giving than taking part in a mere transaction; they want to be connected to the purpose of the ministry. Givers do not want to be objectified and thought of as nothing more than the wallet of the bride of Christ. Henri Nouwen wrote: "When we ask people for money to strengthen or expand the work of the Kingdom, we are also inviting them into a new spiritual communion."[2] And since inviting a proposal from a ministry is the other side of asking for money, a giver who does this is entering into this new shared community.

A friend described it as "a new community of believers that's bigger than ethnicity, bigger than our passport countries, bigger than our education, bigger than the amounts of money we have or are perceived to have or not have." He added: "In this new community, we believe the *fruit* of wise stewardship is *joy*."[3]

Within this communion, the language of have and have not—along with its categorical mindset and practices—is wholly inappropriate to how we relate to each other. In a dysfunctional model of giving, the "poor" receive a trickle-down of resources from the perceived "wealthy." However, when a communion of giving and receiving exists, there are no artificial limits on what can be accomplished, experienced, or exchanged. There can be abundance and scarcity of what is needed for the harvest within all parts of a missional effort. One might involve prayer warriors organized around the world who can be mobilized on short notice, while another raises funds for needed tools and another funds the expertise to use the tools. Each needs the other—and many others as well. We are, after all, engaged in a common task with a common outcome as our goal.

WITHIN THIS COMMUNION OF GIVING AND RECEIVING, THE LANGUAGE OF HAVE AND HAVE NOT IS WHOLLY INAPPROPRIATE TO HOW WE RELATE TO EACH OTHER.

While inviting first-century believers to share in such a communion, the apostle Paul wrote: "At the present time your plenty will supply what they need, so that in turn their plenty will supply what you need. The goal is equality, as it is written: 'The one who gathered much did not have too much, and the one who gathered little did not have too little'" (2 Cor. 8:14–15).

Today, we need a new paradigm of involvement to achieve this communion. This paradigm will equip us to better respond to the wave of majority-world people coming to Christ.

THE WAVE

Body surfing in the Pacific Ocean, bobbing like a cork just beyond foam, you count the waves and wait for the next big swell. You don't think much about the physical forces propelling you forward; you just hope for the ride of your life, and that one more time you can escape being tossed helplessly toward the unforgiving sandy bottom. The trick to getting it right is to be positioned just below the wave's crest, otherwise the wave washes over you. You not only miss the ride, you just mark time in the swells. Get it wrong, and you'll be flung like dirty laundry in a washing machine.

When getting involved with missions, as someone who prays, sends, strategizes, preaches about, invests, fundraises, organizes, tithes, sponsors a child, goes on short-term outreach, volunteers, or simply likes to be thrilled at what God is up to around the world, the swell of our lifetime is here, the wave is cresting, the Son is shining, the water is wonderful.

For the past 2,000 years, these swells have been rolling along. Today, the swell is the combined force of the explosive growth of the church of the majority world. "In 1960, Evangelicals numbered just under 90 million, and by 2010 that had reached close to 600 million."[4] By 2020, two-thirds of Christians will reside in Africa, Asia, and Latin America.[5]

This swell has been generated and has expanded because of the countless number of missionaries and mission organizations that have journeyed to the four points of the compass to preach the good news and do good works. It is also accredited to believers who have joyfully prayed, commissioned, and faithfully

given money to support the work of those who have been in the
fields harvesting.

Near the beginning of the twenty-first century, historian
Philip Jenkins skillfully described this new wave in his book, *The
Next Christendom: The Coming of Global Christianity*. He asserted
that we're living through one of the greatest transformations in
the history of religion worldwide. Over the previous century, he
noted, Christianity had enjoyed explosive growth in the majority world—in Africa, Asia, and Latin America. He contended
that within a few decades, Christianity would be overwhelm-
ingly a non-European, nonwhite religion. We would see no less
than the creation of a new Christendom.[6]

Within this swell, missional entrepreneurs from all of the
pioneer mission fields are now busy working to create the next
swell. We can call them *autochthonous* leaders. I've used words
like *indigenous* or *national* to describe these men and women
in local mission leadership, but these words are imprecise and
can be potentially misleading. So here I'll primarily use *autochthonous*, which can be taken to mean "native to the land." It's a
word that hardly rolls off the tongue, but as we go forward, it will
help us distinguish between missional investors (givers) from
the West and these emerging missional entrepreneurs who seek
partnerships for growing their ministries.

Missional entrepreneurs, like most entrepreneurs, are born
risk-takers. Risk-taking is in the very nature of their calling, if for
no other reason than they are attempting, by definition, something untried and unproven. In the past, the money needed for
missions often came from the West. To seek funds locally meant
starting two new and untried initiatives at the same time. Not

only would the ministry be fundraising where fundraising hadn't been done before, leaders would be doing so while taking on the task of starting a new work from scratch in a potentially difficult environment—perhaps poor, persecuted, or hostile to Christian evangelization. Embedded in risk is the promise of success and its attendant reward. But it wouldn't be true risk if it didn't invite an equal opportunity for dejection and failure.

Getting Started

Michael, an autochthonous leader, is one such risk-taker. He lives and ministers in a dynamic West African nation, beset by extremists. Formerly the seat of a trading empire known for its mathematics, astronomy, literature, and art, the country is mostly Islamic. Only about two percent of its people identify as Christian. Michael is a man on a mission to change that.

Michael wouldn't call himself a leader. He used to own a shop, and he's active in his church and in his local community. A few years ago, he began talking to friends and some of his contacts at neighboring churches, inviting them to plan a sports outreach to young athletes in his city. They began by organizing an informal sports academy, styled after ones they'd learned about in other African settings. It didn't take long before they had a popular ministry demanding more of their volunteer time.

At this point, they came to a fork in the road all missional entrepreneurs face if their work gains some measure of traction and impact. Michael and his team of volunteers were overwhelmed by the demand of the ministry's work. They faced a decision. They could dial it back to be more manageable, or they could organize more formally and grow the ministry. Either decision, in my experience, can be led of God. To grow isn't always necessarily the right thing to do. When seen from the individual beneficiary's point of view, a small, under-funded ministry can be as powerful in impact as a large, well-funded ministry. Size isn't the determiner, faithfulness is. If God leads your ministry to grow, challenges associated with creating an institution are unavoidable. This will involve fundraising, developing a board of directors, acquiring employees, and perhaps even interacting with government agencies.

Michael is sorting through each issue and measuring the risks and rewards with the same pursuit of excellence needed for his business, which produced the income necessary to sustain his family. Nothing less is required of him if he wants to see the survival of the new family of God his ministry is producing. Michael is trusting God for ministry results. He's serving with excellence, and he has faith that God will work through his ministry.

Michael is also taking on a slew of unfamiliar tasks: developing a local board, creating connections to other local congregations, pursuing mission funds in his local setting to supplant the money he was receiving from the West and from his business, and *he is praying*. Progress was slow initially, but his efforts are gaining traction as the Christians in his city learn of a tangible way of expressing their faith to see the gospel spread in their own setting.

However, Michael almost had to stop the work when the local economy experienced a downturn that forced him to close his shop and take a job teaching at the local university as he sought new avenues of funds to keep up with the demand for ministry expansion and his current operations.

After some coaching about the promise of local funding,

rather than try to squeeze additional funds from his few Western friends, he took the plunge. Like the headwaters of a great river, the flow began with a trickle, but now, a number of his watershed rivulets are beginning to form a stream. He is raising local funds for his ministry.

Another risk inherent to many ministries in the majority world involves hostility toward Christians. Michael's work induced risk to the local individuals and churches who were joining him with their time, talent, and money—in a setting of sectarian violence and persecution, they were inviting attention, not only from those who don't want to see the gospel preached, but also from Satan himself. If the ministry is at all successful, Michael and his friends will be snatching souls from Satan's grasp. Yet Michael and his coworkers go right on risking everything in pursuit of their calling. This is real courage and leadership, and his local community of Christians is responding with donations to the vision Michael has cast. For many, it's the first time they've given to missions. Like Michael, they are catching the crest of the wave. They are practicing ownership and engagement and as a result, they are experiencing the communion of giving and receiving.

And like all of us stroking toward the crest of the wave, when we catch it, it is the ride of our life. If we miss the ride because we are temporarily paralyzed by the unfamiliarity of the experience, "no worries," as the saying goes—trying something for the first time is always challenging. You just do what you always do when a new challenge promises great reward: you pick yourself up and try again.

A NEW PARADIGM OF INVOLVEMENT

Michael and thousands like him are the men and women who are awakening to God's call to leadership and to meeting the challenges of sharing the gospel in their own contexts. Like every missional leader for the past two millenniums, they are saying, "God has shown us we've got to do something about the least, the last, and the lost," and they are responding to His call by saying, "Yes, Lord."

AUTOCHTHONOUS MISSIONAL ENTREPRENEURS NEED GIVERS, VOLUNTEERS, PRAYER PARTNERS, AND STAFF.

Like Michael, at some point these autochthonous missional entrepreneurs need givers, volunteers, prayer partners, and possibly staff to join them in their kingdom journey. This seems like pretty standard stuff—it isn't, not even close. The first and foremost reason is the question of money. Where is it? How do they get it? And, in the getting of it, how do they keep their souls and callings safely tucked in God's bosom and His promise of provision? Money is just money, but everything about it as it relates to mission is in flux. For those of us in the West who want to take part in what the Holy Spirit is doing in the majority world, the wave (the tremendous growth of new Christians) calls for a radically new paradigm of involvement—one that disrupts the way we typically think about, work with, and fund missions.

As previously mentioned, this new paradigm involves the ownership and engagement of autochthonous leaders. It is a shift from the operating dynamics of three earlier paradigms of evangelical mission funding, during the eras of Presence, Activity, and Outcomes. Each of these paradigms was reflective of the giving and receiving dynamics of its time and rose to meet the challenges of its generation. And each of the succeeding eras has incorporated the aspects of the previous era into its own.

The Era of Presence

In the nineteenth century, out of revival fervor, evangelical missionaries such as Hudson Taylor and Adoniram Judson were overseas with little more than the prayers of their supporters, along with a theological education and the hope that they would preach the gospel to ears that hadn't yet heard it. They often went to outposts of Western trading companies and businesses and established a base of operations from which they began to do missional activities. They subsisted on their meager savings, their gardens, the hoped-for goodwill of the local merchant community and fellow foreigners, and—most importantly—their faith that God would provide.

Their sending communities saw them as doing God's work overseas, present in the harvest field of the Lord. Communication was limited. Years could pass before the story of their work and what God was doing through them became available to the wider church in the West. Simply, their churches knew them to be "over there." This was *presence*, and it has always been a compelling aspect of mission fundraising. Even today, most Westerners find that raising support for mission work in their homeland, when not going out to a new field, is much harder because there isn't a "go into the world" apparent in their calling.

In those early days of nearly impossible travel and scarce

communication, some of these early mission pioneers ran small enterprises, worked in the local churches serving Western merchants, or took odd jobs to augment their support while they established their outreach. Many suffered incredible deprivation in the cause of the gospel. Yet they prevailed. Many churches they established celebrate their legacy today. So do the missions, schools, and hospitals they established.

Their impact continues in the wide array of justice issues they brought to light when challenging the powers of darkness they encountered. Like many Catholic, Orthodox, and Protestant missionaries who went to unreached peoples and locales before them, the early evangelical missionaries were a living extension of the ministry Jesus began with this announcement: "The Spirit of the Lord is on me, because he has anointed me to proclaim good news to the poor. He has sent me to proclaim freedom for the prisoners and recovery of sight for the blind, to set the oppressed free, to proclaim the year of the Lord's favor" (Luke 4:18–19).

The Era of Activity

In the later years of the nineteenth century, as the wider church embraced these mission accomplishments and travel and communication became easier, a second paradigm of donor and receiver engagement emerged: the Era of *Activity*.

For supporters, easier communication and updates from the field helped bring missions into focus for givers. Missionaries were finally able to communicate about their activities overseas, which encouraged more giving and became a critical element in the fundraising of the day. Activity simply answers the question,

"How is God using you?" The stories of striving to understand the culture and language, translating Scripture, instituting programs—from schools and hospitals to businesses and social justice efforts—and most importantly, sharing the gospel and how people responded, inspired whole new generations to go into the field.

Missionaries from the West were circling the globe, financed by donations raised through personal support and contributions from denominational mission agencies that drew support from member churches.

This model is still commonly illustrated via a world map hung in the foyer of the church and dotted with brightly colored pushpins to mark where the church-supported missionaries are working. A piece of tightly-drawn yarn connects each pushpin to a photograph of the missionary and family or coworkers, accompanied by a card with their names and the focus of their activity in that region. Every few years, the missionaries come through on deputation, featured in a missions weekend event, and share stories of what they're doing to hopefully inspire the congregation to continue its support.

This model is still a dominant method in missions today. Over the last century and a half, it was largely responsible for the incredible growth of evangelicalism in the majority world. It's still responsible for sending thousands of missionaries and millions of dollars overseas from the West. This practice of local churches supporting missionaries is also the dominant model used by a fast-growing cohort of autochthonous mission agencies who are already responsible in our current era for sending out thousands upon thousands of cross-cultural missionaries.

The Era of Outcomes

Then along came the paradigm I first encountered, and, I must admit, championed with some vigor until a few close friends from the majority world decided that gently correcting me was a godlier task than seeking my help as a grant-maker. The Era of *Outcomes* slammed into the world of mission funding in the 1990s. In this paradigm, givers—particularly individual large donors and evangelical foundations—began seeking additional insights into the work of the missions and missionaries they were supporting.

Givers were not only interested in the presence and activity of missions overseas, they now wanted to know the outcomes of the mission activity they were supporting. Some givers were even seeking provable evidence of spiritual outcomes. In its most benign form, the evidence sought was a simple counting of the fruit produced by the funds they were giving.

This is not as easy as it may seem. First, it begs the question: What is fruit? Is it baptisms for an evangelist, disciples for a pastor, or perhaps a useful measurement of churches planted? Of course, the latter then begs the question: what is a church?

I once encountered a small autochthonous missions team that said they planted a church a day by walking into the center of a village mid-day and telling the gospel story. When they got halfway through the story, they would stop and say, "If you want to hear more, meet us by a tree just outside the village." There, they told the rest of the gospel story and presented the plan of salvation to whoever showed up. They then formed a church from those who had committed their life to Christ and appointed the villager who had asked the best questions to be the pastor.

They gave the villagers some tapes to get started with and told the congregation they would return within a month to begin discipling them. I'm not sure if their model actually worked in every village they visited, but they counted each as having a church.

Simple counting, no matter what you were counting—churches, baptisms or salvations—didn't seem enough for givers. This only prompted other questions: "Are you being effective? Are you measuring and evaluating your activities? (And even more difficult to determine), are other organizations getting better results with less funding?"

This demand for a reporting of results did, however, bring a needed corrective to what, in some cases, had been a lack of clearly defined goals. But it also meant that overseas missions had to offer evidence of conformity to modern Western management practices before they could obtain funding from Western grant-makers and church missions committees.

In the granting community, there was a noticeable drift toward accepting self-fulfilling proposals. This comes about when the very questions leaders are asked become the very thing they try to accomplish. The danger is apparent: the giver is driving the strategies, perhaps at the expense of the ministry's calling from God. Perennial confusion about what could be accurately measured and how to do so ushered in a bewildering round of conferences, academic papers, and books that continues today.

This demand for reporting outcomes led to a debilitating chasm of cynicism between people on the same side of the mission to share the gospel. One majority-world leader told me, "In the eighties, we were evangelists, and the donors seemed happy. In the nineties, they wanted us to be church planters, so we planted churches, and they seemed happy. Since 2000, they've wanted us to undertake holistic ministry—helping people while we evangelized them and planted churches—so we became holistic whiz kids, and they seemed happy. In all these cases, we did nothing different from what we'd always been doing." His frustration was evident.

Additionally, even the cherished tradition of long-term commitments to Western missionaries began to waver. Missionaries were dropped from the regular support of churches that increasingly were pulling back from supporting their denominational mission structures and were spending more of their mission budgets on their own programs, including an increased emphasis on short-term missions. With this shift, givers began moving their funding from missionary support to *project* support, the results of which were easier to track.

And of course, this led to more and more givers traveling to see the field, which led to more questions. It didn't take long for a collective headache to begin encroaching on those in long-term missions. The increased emphasis on reports and measurable results brought unintended consequences. Within a few years, allegations of falsified field reports began to tarnish the reputations of even highly respected mission organizations and leaders. Some missions created extrapolated research. An example of the kind of thinking behind this uncertain process of estimation might be: "If a certain church planter plants one church a month, and there are twelve other church planters, that means twelve churches are being planted each month. Let's state that in our proposal, and since our missionaries raise their own support, we have little to no fundraising costs. We pay our office significantly lower wages than the private sector, so we can claim low over-head as well. Let's report that also."

Seems out of bounds, doesn't it? Yet all of these cobbled-together claims were communicated to me verbatim. Unfortunately, because the "power" appears to be with givers, fund seekers provide these types of answers to appease supporters who aren't aware of the complexity of reporting outcomes. Yet, as those who experienced this paradigm know, a lot of good came out of that time as well as a few things that needed to be corrected. In fact, the overarching idea of a communion of giving and receiving was a direct result of significant efforts to correct outcomes-based funding. And just in the nick of time, because concurrent to those developments the next era rolled in.

The Era of Ownership and Engagement

A decade or so before Jenkins's *The Next Christendom* defined for us the new reality we were facing with the explosive growth of Christianity, many of us involved in evangelical mission philan-thropy began to sense the potential strength of Christian autoch-thonous leaders. At the time, we used the word *indigenization* to describe this paradigm of *ownership* and *engagement* by local leaders.

In the mid-1990s at First Fruit, we called it the "Success Paradox." On one hand, we considered it a success to be making an increasing number of grants to autochthonous organizations, though these grants usually involved a lot more discovery work and smaller dollar amounts owing to smaller operating budgets. On the other hand, Western grants to autochthonous organiza-tions headquartered overseas were harder to make than larger dollar grants to typical Western missions. They were also harder to find. We had to go where they were and sort through cultural dynamics to adjust to their context as much as we needed them to adjust to ours. Familiarity was the course of the day with Western-headquartered missions, no matter who the leader was.

When I started traveling to the overseas ministries we were seeking to fund in the early 1980s, many of the leaders I was introduced to had never met a representative of an American philanthropy. Yet, what they didn't know about me paled in comparison to what I didn't know about them, since often, I only had some pages ripped from an old Fodor's guide and my dog-eared copy of *Operation World* to brief me. The topic of money wasn't even the biggest hurdle—expectations were. Often, neither party knew what the other was assuming or planning. I coached them on how to write proposals my board could fund, and, along with patiently mentoring me, they helped me understand the challenges of spreading the gospel where they were working. They bore the burden of educating me with the joy that became a communion of giving and receiving, including, at the most primary level, trying not to create dependency, much less resentment and confusion, while trying to serve each other.

WHERE THE AUTOCHTHONOUS CHURCH IS STRONG, IT HAS ACHIEVED SELF-GOVERNING, SELF-FINANCING, AND SELF-PROPAGATING, EVEN IN THE FACE OF DEBILITATING FINANCIAL POVERTY.

I've observed that where the autochthonous church is strong, it has achieved some version of what is called the three-self model—meaning that churches are self-governing, self-financing, and self-propagating, despite debilitating financial poverty. Often these churches have undergone a difficult transition; they're no longer dependent on the funds brought through a foreign support base.

As autochthonous missional entrepreneurs like Michael take more and more responsibility for missions within their own contexts, this paradigm disrupts the long-established ways of funding missions. We've entered the Era of *Ownership and Engagement* when majority-world Christian leaders, rather than Western missionaries and boards, own their mission efforts, including governance, finance, results, and growth. And they proactively engage as full and equal partners with anyone coming alongside them on their journey to accomplish their calling. Western givers, no matter the size of the donation they intend to make,

THERE'S REAL SPIRITUAL POWER IN THE CONCEPT OF OWNERSHIP AND ENGAGEMENT.

should give heed to this new paradigm. Daniel, the Romanian with the old gym socks, and the Egyptian did, and look where it got them.

There's real spiritual power in this concept of ownership and engagement. As these leaders are able to develop local resources, they bring in the covering and fellowship of their fellow Christians nearby who join the good fight for souls. As these local believers and the churches they attend exercise generosity (in many cases out of abject financial poverty) and invest their money into the work, they share ownership and responsibility for the work. This fellowship builds strength, and strength builds confidence. And confidence is attractive to future partners.

Everywhere I've traveled, I've seen churches supported by their local congregations; however, in the past, the first few generations of many of these churches were dependent on their Western founders for their missional outreaches. Now, in this post-colonial era, they are self-sustaining in the core operations of their missional work and can invite outside participation as true equals. Sustained interdependence exists when each partner—giver, receiver, or agency—works together and is financially sustained for their own core operations within a local context. This may be easy for givers depending on the source of their money, but, nonetheless, their money can accomplish nothing without the partner who is seeking the transformative effect of the gospel in the fields where they work. This need for sustained interdependence is also true for the ministry or individual seeking to realize Kingdom goals. The transformation they seek, that also attracts givers, needs resources to be accomplished. In this era, to achieve ownership and engagement, the autochthonous leader must first seek a communion of giving and receiving within his or her own local setting.

This then sets the stage for a true and equal partnership in a cross-cultural or international setting, where each offers the other what they need in pursuit of their mutual callings. When this happens, the partnership goes beyond mere financial transaction and lays the foundation for a transformative communion of giving and receiving across cultures and vast financial gaps.

And now, we come to the biggest challenge in this new paradigm.

The Money Question

When beginning the journey toward a God-directed calling to funding or working in missions, the money question is the one that usually trips up the missional entrepreneur first. Just about everything else seems doable, even if only on a small scale. But when the inevitable question arises, "Where will my help come from?" faith turns a calling into accomplishment.

Yet, the question is valid, and it must be asked . . . but it should be asked *last*. Ask it first, and you might limit your ability to imagine and dream about the scope of your ministry. Ignore the question, and you risk being like the man who began to build his house but ran out of funds before putting the roof on. Raising the question last puts it where it can be asked most easily. By then, you'll likely have done some planning and formed a reasonable idea of a required initial budget. You'll know the strategies you want to begin with, and you might even have a good sense of how to communicate with others what you want to accomplish.

ESPECIALLY FOR A MAJORITY-WORLD MISSIONAL ENTREPRENEUR, THE MONEY QUESTION ALWAYS LOOMS LARGE.

Especially for a majority-world missional entrepreneur, the money question—regardless of when it's asked—always looms large. And a great temptation lies before both the funder and the fundraiser. In places where most autochthonous leaders are following their calling, in areas where a low base of cash and wealth exists, or where there may be wealth but a mature stewardship culture has not yet developed, the best-run, best-funded ministries may well be led by Westerners or by a local indigenous leader solely funded by Western sources.

This presents a discouraging challenge for even the most optimistic and forward-looking missional entrepreneur. If Westerners appear to be the only ones with money, the autochthonous leader is tempted to ask, "Where's my American?" But such thinking is based on some lingering wrong assumptions.

Particularly harmful is the stubborn belief that the money is in the West. While that was largely true years ago, times have changed. In recent years, a large number of ministries founded by Western agencies have received a "sustainability letter" announcing a pullback of Western financial support, along with the suggestion that the ministry come up with a "sustainability strategy" for funding its continued work.

I have a Latin American friend—well-versed in fundraising and management practices—who was approached by leaders of a prominent seminary in his country. They had just received such a letter from their sponsoring agency in the United States. With alarm, the seminary's leaders were staring into a future of steep cutbacks in faculty support, scholarship funding, and publishing and curriculum development projects. My friend helped them understand that American evangelical givers in the second decade of the twenty-first century have been turning their attention away from Latin America toward less evangelized fields. The seminary was being forcibly ushered into this new Era of Ownership and Engagement. They'll have to build their own fundraising operation in pursuit of local funds, and until they find them, they'll have to severely trim back their programs. This is not a one-off situation; much of my coaching and that of my colleagues centers on the struggle for sustainability. The answer can be found in our worship communities everywhere in the world, not merely in our giving, but in our preaching.

Hudson Taylor, the nineteenth-century missionary who pioneered evangelical missions in China, laid out the cause of a communion of giving and receiving in his paper (written to the whole Christian church), "To Every Creature." He called for urgent action on four fronts: "First, prayer for one thousand evangelists for China; second, 'united, simultaneous action by the whole body' of Christians; third, intelligent cooperation to avoid neglect in one region or duplication in another; fourth, sacrificial giving by churches and individuals in support of their missions."[7]

This simple approach is as powerful today as when Taylor first laid it out. If gospel-preaching congregations embrace these disciplines today—and every individual who says Jesus is Lord will carry them out, how much further will the darkness be rolled back?

Come on, surf the swell. The water is great. Jump in!

When Money Goes on Mission

. . . it serves the loving actions of the gospel.
When there is a communion of giving and
receiving, the exchange of money goes
from a mere transaction to a transformative
relationship of fellowship and equality at
the foot of the cross between those who go,
give, and send.

LIVING STONES

The Foundation of Sustained
Interdependence

IN MANY GREAT and ancient civilizations, there was, at one time or another, a despot so full of himself that he drafted the poor souls from the despised of his culture to do the hard labor of preparing him a massive grave befitting his ego. Despite the fact that I can't help but think about the poor indentured workers who gave up their lives so their king could cross the River Styx or get to wherever he thought he was headed with his stuff, I also can't help but admire the craftsmanship, ingenuity, and just the massive scale of these projects. What were the tax levies like? Yikes!

So, when traveling in Egypt for the third time, I finally visited one of the seven wonders of the ancient world, the Great Pyramid of Giza. It is a profoundly simple structure; essentially, layered blocks of hewn limestone stacked one upon another that create an astonishing sight. In viewing the structure, it was easy to grasp the crucial importance of the foundation, built with a perfect cornerstone by those ancient artisans and craftsmen.

Likewise, a ministry that possesses true ownership and

engagement and that seeks sustainability must be built upon a solid foundation. The ministry's cornerstone is nothing less than Jesus Himself; we anchor the ministry structure on Him, as He keeps the plumb-line true. And He provides the hewn foundation stones—*living stones, His people* (1 Peter 2:5) to build a true foundation with their gifts. The vital strength of each of these stones isn't the amount of money represented in any particular gift nor the amount of money people give cumulatively; rather, *the strength of the structure is in the simple act of giving.*

In essence, it is the connection that goes past the transaction to the transformation of all involved—the giver, the missionary, and the beneficiary of the loving action—in God's economy. Every instance of heartfelt giving to the ministry from every source—elders, congregations, business people, the young and the old, the wealthy and the impoverished, even widows and orphans—gives strength to the ministry. Even the smallest gift, like the Romanian's gift of old gym socks, imparts inestimable strength, if for no other reason than his or her gift is precious in God's sight, as it should be also in ours.

In God's economy, what counts is not the giver's amount, but the giver's faithfulness, sacrifice, and prayer. A primary case in point is that of someone our Lord observed:

> Jesus sat down opposite the place where the offerings were put and watched the crowd putting their money into the temple treasury. Many rich people threw in large amounts. But a poor widow came and put in two very small copper coins, worth only a few cents.
>
> Calling his disciples to him, Jesus said, "Truly I tell you,

this poor widow has put more into the treasury than all the others. They all gave out of their wealth; but she, out of her poverty, put in everything—all she had to live on." (Mark 12:41–44)

This widow with her few pennies became the most celebrated donor in history. Why? Jesus says it's because she put in more than all the others: she gave sacrificially. Hers was the joyful act of giving. There's untold strength in that joy.

We don't read in this scene that Jesus ran over to this woman to say, "No, dear one, take your money back home; you need it more than the temple does." He didn't tell her that because she *wanted* to give. And Jesus honored her for it.

Local donations are like this—no matter the relative financial status of the communities from which they're raised, they impart a fibrous and enduring strength that always extends from the true giver. At the Rescue Mission, where I first learned this, our foundation was established on the strength of our small donations. At the time, I didn't know how to raise large dollar gifts, and I was thankful for our financial partners who were predominantly almost as poor as the Mission. Even in a severe economic downturn, they kept up their sacrificial giving. The strength they imparted was the Mission's foundation.

By participating in God's work through our acts of giving, we express our faith and devotion toward God. It is *worship*. These acts of worship bind giver and receiver together in the pursuit of a common cause, carried forward by God to fulfill a calling imparted by Him.

Layer upon layer, when a foundation of living stones is built and local giving grows stronger, a paradox emerges because the stronger local giving is, the more attractive the ministry's work will be to a much wider realm of potential givers—even internationally. International givers will actually seek out such ministries and will want to come alongside local giving communities.

I experienced this early in my Christian philanthropic employment when I became aware of the Friends Missionary Prayer Band in India. This ministry began during an extraordinary period of growth of Christianity in the mid-twentieth century among the "graduates" of vacation Bible schools in India's southernmost state of Tamil Nadu. Deeply impacted by their new faith, these graduates created prayer groups that later began sending missionaries and producing a series of newsprint magazines about God's work in the pioneering fields of the Lord in the north of India.

In the mid-1980s, I discovered their magazine and read it with prayerful excitement whenever their all-too-infrequent issues arrived. I was fascinated by stories of the growth of the ministry from initially a few missionaries to more than five hundred sent out by the mid-1990s. Each issue I read detailed even more growth and spiritual impact. This whetted my appetite, as a grant-maker, to meet these folks to explore getting involved with a gift.

This turned out to be harder than I imagined; the ministry actually had a rule against accepting outside gifts. Instead, they were committed to the self-governing, self-propagating, self-funding model of missions. Their missionaries were expected to be funded by their home churches and by "prayer bands," which were composed of small fellowships of prayer and financial supporters scattered throughout the southern states of India where the gospel had first been preached by, who is believed to have been, the apostle Thomas.

Later, remaining rooted to the idea of local giving, the churches the ministry planted were to finance the sending of their own missionaries. Their sacrificial giving of even meager amounts of money gave the mission the foundational strength to grow.

In less than a couple of decades, their field teams sparked a wildfire of evangelization and church planting among upper-caste Hindus as well as Dalits, considered the "lowest" people group in India's caste system.

A few years earlier I had encountered the pervasive idea among many Christian funders that the gospel went to Northern India to die. I knew several funders who had figuratively shaken the dust off their feet and had turned away from this vast and not yet ripe harvest and had decided not to fund in India. The opposite was true for me. When I came to Christ, I experienced revival first hand. I was fascinated by the Friends Missionary Prayer Band's reports because they were describing what I had experienced. And it was happening in India, a country I had been told was a graveyard in missions.

The first mentor who helped me to unmask this fallacy was Dave Bennett. Through his mentoring and his books, derived from his years of academic study of the Indian church, I became determined to break the fog of my ignorance of India. I sought a meeting with Patrick Joshua, general secretary of Friends Missionary Prayer Band. Despite all of the advantages of my position to undertake such a pursuit, my plans came up miserably short as other opportunities drew my attention away.

But God had His own plan.

The ministry continued to grow, and it created a demand to start social action outreaches where they had planted new fellowships, such as medical clinics, schools, and jobs programs. Though they had sustained their growth by adhering to the principles of local funding, they now found themselves needing additional money to accomplish new demands for programmatic growth. What they needed now were the kind of grants I could facilitate through First Fruit. I didn't know it then, but I was about to have a go at entering into a genuine communion of giving and receiving with Patrick and his mission.

Incongruously, it happened at a COMIBAM conference in Mexico in 1997 that brought together leaders from virtually all of the autochthonous Latin American mission movements. Patrick was there to invite Latin American agencies to send missionaries to India.

I didn't know who he was until I heard him speak. After the plenary session ended, I found Patrick sitting alone in the bleachers of the cavernous meeting hall, and I introduced myself, telling him I'd been reading their news magazine and was wondering if there was a way for First Fruit to partner with the ministry. I made plans with him to visit the mission's headquarters in India, and I was looking forward to facilitating First Fruit to come alongside them.

A few weeks later, when I arrived at his office in Chennai, known then as Madras, I could tell he was unsure how to greet me. They'd never hosted a representative of an American evangelical philanthropy. There was much we had to learn about working with each other. At the time, I hadn't really pondered the negative impact large international gifts can have on a dynamic, locally supported mission. Thankfully, Patrick had carefully considered this, and he took on the task of helping me to understand how to properly help his ministry without harming the core ownership and engagement principles that were the bedrock of his mission. When both he and I got it right—that is, when I knew how to trust him to use First Fruit's gift of God's money, and he learned how to offer the accountability I needed for my board's assurance that their gift was meeting expectations—we then entered into a sacred space where we, and all involved with us, experienced the communion of giving and receiving.

THE COMPASSION PARADOX

Previously, I mentioned the Success Paradox, which is framed by the idea that it's easier to make a large gift in your own culture than a small one when working across cultures. And if it is your calling to work across cultures, then understanding that you must solve this paradox is one of the first steps toward a communion of giving and receiving. To do this, perhaps begin by asking yourself Brian Fikkert's implied question in his book, *When Helping Hurts*[1]: "How can I help and not hurt?" Truly seek the answer and you will discover where the paradox is hampering you from achieving true communion with your partners who receive your gifts as they work to see you as a partner and not just as a source of money.

While embracing the changes that must occur to achieve a communion of giving and receiving, to ameliorate the challenge of the Success Paradox, you might find you are hampered by another, more hidden challenge. I call it the Compassion Paradox, or finding a balance between the heartbeat (the passion) and the brainwave (the process) of a gift, because all gifts have them, no matter how small or large.

In Matthew 25, we see the simple act of giving a cup of cold water to a thirsty man is the same as giving it to Jesus. What could be a deeper act of worship than this? In cross-cultural giving, this means the resource that is given—whether time, talent, or money—is given so that someone else can carry out a loving action on the giver's behalf.

On the surface, this can seem nothing more than giving a gift and trusting that it will be used as intended. However, no matter the size of the gift, solving the Compassion Paradox means understanding the heartbeat and the brainwave that characterize the gift and working toward a balance. This works best when the giver and receiver work diligently with truth and grace to communicate clearly. While love compels our hearts to action, our brains must be engaged at the same time. We must wisely think through the implications of our gifts. Perhaps because of my experience at the Rescue Mission, when I first thought of this, the picture that formed in my mind was of a few of us walking down a street and encountering a homeless man sprawled on the stoop of a closed restaurant, begging for food. My first thought, if I was feeling missional, possibly might have been, "If there's one, there's bound to be more, so let's build a kitchen."

This thought represents a brainwave, or a strategy, to fix an underlying problem. However, a more action-oriented, rather than process-oriented, individual might jab me in the ribs and correctly ask, "What about this one, this man right here?" This desire to move in compassion and immediacy represents a heartbeat reaction.

At First Fruit, we actually elevated this concept to an operating principle—that all the grants we presented to the board for their consideration would be characterized by a brainwave and a heartbeat, sometimes with a lean toward one direction. It was always a challenge, a positive tension, to find the compassion and strategic balance necessary for an institutional-sized grant. Let's look at an example.

A ministry working in community development programs wants to help tenant farmers who are at the mercy of greedy middle men. To solve the challenge, the ministry decides to buy a truck so the farmers can take their produce directly to whatever market is offering the best prices. The brainwave of the grant is the strategy of buying the truck and considering all it means to the local economy. The heartbeat is in the ability of the farmers to gain control of their livelihood and to find the fullness of life that God has for them.

The stuff of mission is ordinary. They needed a truck. The outcome of mission is extraordinary; they gained a measure of control over their futures that might have otherwise eluded them.

I've worked on such grants, and I have found the outcome is always more interesting than the process. This is true of some of the most modest gifts in cross-cultural giving; for example, child sponsorship. A compassionate person, let's say living in California, can, for the cost of a modest meal in a restaurant, feed a hungry child in an impoverished country for a month. Of course, to do so, he or she needs an agency to inform him or her that such a thing is possible and how to do it. The promise in the transaction is that a child will be fed. This is the heartbeat. Hardly any mention is made of the incredible amount of work it takes to make sure the gift accomplishes this promise. It is a situation rife with challenge. The agency has to hire an astonishing array of people to get that simple loving action accomplished. Holding accountable whoever received the gift on behalf of the child is the very tension inherent in the Compassion Paradox. Because it is not easy, some have given up trying.

Fikkert, in a recent article, bemoaned an unintended consequence of his widely read book. A troubling number of people—not understanding the title *When Helping Hurts*—misinterpreted it to mean they should stop funding overseas missions. "I want to see the opposite," Fikkert says. "I want to see much more money going to mission."[2]

He is right. Americans should be the most generous of people, and we flatter ourselves that we are, but relatively few among us give like the widow. Guilt is useless as an antidote. We are only to give from a joyful and generous heart, and despite the decline in American missions giving—and in church giving for that matter[3]—the generous heart of believers who give to missions is evident. The question of giving more, and more sacrificially, is not just the fruit of generosity; done thoughtfully, it unleashes the tremendous potential for missions giving embedded in every Christian population worldwide.

For givers to be helpful, they should dig a little deeper in thought, not money, and look for the brainwave and heartbeat when considering a gift. Doing so may help them more deeply connect to the impact of the gift.

This is no different when making a large institutional foundation grant. The critical issue is the changing dynamic of the mission funding paradigms. For example, some ministries funded by international donors have limited autonomy, often with what may be large budgets in their own settings but which are small compared to similar Western organizations doing the same work. Often these semi-autochthonous organizations are really only subsidiary programs of their Western givers. These missions, I've found, often accomplish dynamic ministry outcomes under the most severe conditions in almost complete financial deprivation. It is these circumstances that make the mission and its beneficiaries so compelling as an object of generosity. The Compassion Paradox then compels us to ask the questions, "Could this mission be more effective with not only more resources but with more resources that are given in a more thoughtful manner? Could they be far more effective with a local donor base? Are they mortgaging their future for the present?" These are brainwave questions.

Over the past few years, I've coached several American givers who've experienced donor fatigue after having become ensnared as the main source of support for some semi-autonomous missions. They ask me how the circle of givers can be expanded. This question, in any of its forms, causes me to ask, "Why not expand the donor base where the work is?" One of these good-hearted givers once told me, "That's unthinkable!" My reply was, "Well, I'm thinking it!"

I'll grant it's easier to raise money in the United States than it is in most any mission field. I knew the above-mentioned giver wanted to expand their donor base out of his pure compassion.

He didn't want to hold back the mission he was supporting. He was operating not only out of compassion, but also with the strong belief that with focused resources, anything was possible. But as the ministry he was supporting continued to grow, he and other givers couldn't imagine not being obligated in some manner to help.

Of course, money is a significant part of growth—allowing increases in staff, facilities, programs, and aiding distribution, but it is not the reason for growth. No, growth is a spiritual issue. The undiscovered givers in the local mission's setting are the fuel for real growth in all of its dimensions. When they are discovered and they give, they are the living stones of a great foundation that will serve and will be a source of growth for generations to come.

As cross-cultural givers, it is important that we not deny those we give to the discipleship and joy that comes from their own giving. I've never encountered more generosity than I have seen among the poorest of Christians. When they give, like us, they experience the same understanding of trusting in God and they also experience the resultant joy of giving. This is at the heartbeat of encouraging local giving. Likewise, the brainwave of encouraging local giving has to do with their participation in prayer and the establishment of local accountability. In their participation in this way—no matter its impact on the bottom line—these people's discipleship, worship, and thankfulness might actually be more critical for the mission's growth than any of its more commonly perceived ministry aspects.

As we encounter successful ministry in the field where the ownership and engagement paradigm has yet to be evident, we often find ourselves walking in the steps of very spiritually successful missions that really just need to adjust to their own success.

Establishing ownership and engagement should be encouraged by those of us in the West. The autochthonous leader must embrace the resultant chaos that always accompanies major change. Then they must cast vision, and mission must be preached from the pulpits. Only then can true and equal partnership occur.

Responsibility

We can find these opportunities to encourage ownership and engagement everywhere we look. It could be a need for clean water in a village where children are dying from a parasitical illness, or for overcoming the power of spiritual darkness in a place where the gospel hasn't been widely preached. Such situations tug at our hearts and often cause us to want to respond financially. These things should lead us to the question, "Is my gift funding an appropriate solution to the real situation?"

If you're a large financial giver, you might be able to pay for installing a well or building a health clinic in a faraway village or funding a team for a year to preach and establish churches in a distant region. But would these be the wisest grants? Are they compatible with local circumstances and the ability of autochthonous ministries to be effective? Could there be a better way to give?

In my years of considering these questions with givers while preparing to make recommendations for gifts, I've learned that each grant presents such a unique set of circumstances that surprising discoveries can be made when trying to understand how the gift will be effective.

A former executive with a relief and development organization told me about his time in a remote African village with a well-drilling crew. One hot, dusty afternoon, the crew was taking measurements and beginning to drill test holes. Observing this activity, my friend stood under a nearby shade tree with several villagers. Through an interpreter, he asked them what they thought of the drilling team and their work. The answer startled him. "These are very clever witch doctors," they said, calling attention especially to the mysterious looking instruments and tools in the workers' hands.

By the end of the day, the drilling came up dry. Startled that they were thought of as witch doctors, the team, although now nervous about how they were viewed, started fresh the next day at a nearby site. This time they struck water.

My friend was again watching the work with the villagers, and he asked what they thought of the team's success. The villagers informed him, "We knew how much you wanted this well to work, so last night we made a sacrifice to the river god, so you would succeed." The team's work had only validated the villagers' animistic worldview, which wasn't quite what the organization and my friend had in mind. That might not have been the case if a nearby autochthonous ministry had been brought in as an ongoing partner, empowered not only to lead the effort but to be a self-sustaining agent of follow-up actions. This ministry was doing its best to answer Jesus' question about bringing Him a cup of cold water when He was thirsty (Matt. 25), but perhaps they could have done it in a better way.

This was done well in a similar ministry I encountered years ago led by one of my heroes Bill Ashe, who founded Lifewater, a ministry that, at the time, sent volunteer hydrologists and well-diggers to locales around the world to establish wells on church properties for needy villages. Because there was already a witness, they were freed to focus on other critical issues. As they launched into the work, they learned that digging a well wasn't enough; there was more to do. Villagers needed to learn rudimentary health practices as well. There was also the matter of maintaining and repairing the wells and using technology appropriate to the area, so that maintenance and repair could be accomplished with local resources and skills when the hydrologists and well experts left. This led to a whole new project of setting up local pump shops in the districts where wells were dug.

Then more questions needed to be answered. What parts of this work could be done by local Christians and churches? More fundamentally, was clean water the biggest need in these settings? What about the gospel? What if a targeted village was as ripe for a harvest of souls as it was for a new well? These questions caused this ministry to begin doing spiritual assessments of the villages where they were drawn to work and to seek out partnerships with those who could more effectively preach the gospel and plant churches. Today, led by Justin Narducci, Lifewater has grown by equipping village councils to lead and maintain water health programs for themselves.

In another challenge, considering the Compassion Paradox, we learn that the obvious solution isn't always the best thing to pursue first. This is a common enough problem, but when it means life and death, it takes on another different sort of urgency.

Some years ago in Asia, I visited a massive landfill. In connection with a project First Fruit had funded, I was there alongside a young missionary named Steven. Five years earlier, Steven had come to the landfill to see what he could do for the tens of thousands of trash pickers who literally lived on the dump and in the perpetual haze of smoke that engulfed the rotting mess. He'd learned that children on the dump—as one would expect in such an environment—were dying from preventable diseases. But as he walked about and interacted with families, he became aware that preventing death wasn't the most immediate problem on the minds of the adults. Burying the dead was.

These people felt that their loved ones, no matter the circumstances of their life, deserved and needed a proper funeral as they went to their next life. Nearby funeral directors were providing the service only at outrageous costs, often as much as thousands of dollars.

People in the dump developed a unique way of raising the necessary money for these funerals. When someone died, the body was placed on the roof of the family's shed-like home, which was the signal for a floating dice game to begin. It would go on until the family, taking a percentage of each dice roll, had raised enough money to purchase the funeral services.

Although Steven wanted to establish a clinic for inoculations at the dump, he struck upon the idea of creating a local business (through a willing funeral home) to provide funerals at less than $300 for these families. The idea worked. By providing this service, Steven won the people's hearts, opening them up to understanding the need for the clinic. In the end, they helped him establish the clinic, to the point of building a concrete building on top of the dump. Early childhood death dropped by nearly 90 percent, and more than a dozen churches were built throughout the dump. Steven and his fellow missionaries helped dozens of families start micro-businesses.

As I walked the dump with Steven, I heard people affectionately calling him "Doctor."

It took a grant to help Steven establish the clinic and supply it with medicines. However, the last time I was there, the work was completely self-sustained by the dozen or so churches located on the dump. Love—meeting people at the point of their felt need—did the work.

The Unrealized Power of Local Support

In the mid-1990s, I was in Costa Rica with my family for a year, serving with the highly successful Christo para la Ciudad (Christ for the City) mission. Early on during this time, I was invited to a Christian businessmen's lunch; for more than twenty years, the group had been gathering weekly in downtown San Jose for a noontime study of the Bible. As I arrived, I noticed others arriving for the lunch who were driving BMWs, Mitsubishi SUVs, and Mercedes-Benzes. They carried brick-size cell phones and snapped these down on the table in front of them in case they had to take an important call. The scene could have been happening in the wealthy city of Newport Beach, California.

Later, returning to the office, I asked the team, "How much money do you raise here in Costa Rica for your annual budget?" They told me that local resources provided only $5,000 of their $300,000 annual budget.

"What about these local businessmen? Do you raise money from them?"

"No," they said.

"Don't you respect them? Why aren't you asking for their help in your work?"

One of the team members looked at me thoughtfully and said, "Let's try." He was the staff member responsible for these weekly lunch meetings and within three weeks, he had organized a breakfast meeting for these businessmen at a nice hotel. It was the first time they had gathered to consider the question of funding the mission they had benefited from over the years. He then presented them with a list of their programs and needs. Those businessmen gave $30,000 that morning, and eventually took on full responsibility for the entire annual budget for Christ for the City in Costa Rica.

Sometimes if you push a little bit on a closed door, it pops open. At First Fruit, we funded a Western ministry called CURE, which provides orthopedic hospitals for children. The long-term funding model for each hospital is centered on a two-tiered patient system; patients and families who can afford care will cover enough of the hospital costs so that those who can't pay can still be helped. Once the hospital is up and running, which usually takes a couple of years, it moves toward becoming self-supporting. It's a sustainable model that has proven viable all over the world.

CURE's Craig Hammon came to First Fruit to request a large grant for the second year of funding for their new hospital in Zambia. Before promoting the grant to my board, I asked their team if they could first raise $25,000 in local funding from local Zambians. Though they had no precedent for this, they agreed to try it.

Six weeks later, I received a photograph of a local Zambian

businessman, the owner of the capital city's Toyota dealership. He was holding a huge cardboard check for $15,000. Before long, the Zambians had raised the additional money and had their second year of operations covered. This was a blended funding strategy that helped their hospital establish their base of living stones.

Engaging as Equals

There has never been a time when God hasn't encouraged His people's generosity, with whatever they have, to help those in need wherever they're found.

It's vitally important that we understand the funding dynamics in this new Era of Ownership and Engagement. As autochthonous leaders take on full responsibility for their work and establish a foundation of local living stones, they're prepared to engage as equals with whoever might want to help with their work. This is the essence of stepping away from the paternalistic over dog/underdog approach in funding, with its endemic failures and crushing impact on dynamic growth.

Engagement as equals, where it hasn't existed before, requires a process of creating new definitions and new ways of relating to each other—equally on both sides of the relationship. If anyone approaches this relationship with the assumption that wealth defines importance, the relationship will never be right. In God's economy, money defines neither leadership nor position. It just buys stuff. Necessary stuff. Money is a tool, like a chisel and hammer; but it is not the stones, the living stones that are each measured from the perfect cornerstone (Jesus), which was not hewn by human hands.

When Money Goes on Mission

... local funding builds community support and generates local accountability between the church and ministry.

TRUST AND ACCOUNTABILITY

Fruitful Giving and
Receiving at the Foot of the Cross

EIGHT THOUSAND feet up a trail, in the High Sierras of California—after fasting on the hike up and sharing communion with a friend and another person whom I think might have been an angel—I clearly heard from God, again. The stirring in my spirit deepened rather than abated. God was reinforcing my call into ministry . . . and I was afraid.

Nearly two years earlier, I had heard the same message just as clearly as I did that night on the mountain, and my reaction was the same . . . all I wanted to do was the opposite of what I clearly understood God was asking me to do. Was I born under the "sign" of Jonah? I questioned God, thinking, "You want me to do what?"

His call ignited my fears: of poverty (the Rescue Mission was terribly unfunded), my loss of status (like I had any to begin with), and most importantly, that no one would want to marry me if I worked there. These were perfectly good grounds for not following God's call, I reasoned.

I didn't know that night in the mountains that a few weeks later, in my finest nanosecond of existence, I would say yes to His call and that it would be a hinge point in time of dying to myself. The weekend hike occurred because I had encountered the strange phenomena of being troubled in my spirit, not in my heart, nor my head, and I really didn't recognize it for what it truly was. God was getting my attention in His unmistakable way.

When saying yes, I instantly experienced what might be called a backbone replacement. I sat straight up from my prostrate supplication and haven't looked back since. And it all happened because in that moment of *communion with God*, I was as vulnerable before Him as I had been since the very moment of my conversion.

COMMUNION WITH GOD IS THE FOUNDATION OF OUR FELLOWSHIP WITH ONE ANOTHER AND THE LAUNCHING POINT OF TRUE PARTNERSHIP IN ANY KINGDOM VENTURE.

When you are truly communing with God and hear His voice and sense His direction, it is an awesome and awful reminder of what our salvation costs and what is possible because of it. In turn, communion is also at the foundation of our fellowship with one another and should be the launching point of true partnership in any Kingdom venture, whether you are participating as an investor, giver, volunteer, staff member, or leader.

Communion is a time of coming together, intimacy, partaking of a common meal, remembrance, and hopefully, a clean slate. When I resisted God's leading, my fears were a barrier to my communion with God. Barriers to communing with God and each other are all around and affect all of us.

Here's how some barriers have played out in the funding of missions...

It's fair to say that the pursuit of measurable outcomes in missions (mentioned earlier) was well intentioned, but it created barriers with those working in the field. On one hand, successful Western business leaders who have set aside a significant portion of their wealth as an offering are accustomed to applying rigorous accountability to their investment decisions. In their business, they need real-time indicators of how they are doing, not anecdotal indicators, but hard and fast numbers, progress markers, evaluations, and reports. Yet, the mission work they like to fund—which is fiercely dedicated to loving the least, the last, and the lost and is serving in the toughest places—faces a difficult challenge trying to define results in the language and methods common to business.

And right here is the rub. Is it possible to find common ground?

At the emergence of the outcomes era, there was a broad perception that administrative efficiency was far more developed in the business arena than in missions. With their typical business backgrounds, many Western givers responding to significant-sized proposals tended to evaluate a mission's operations according to the business environment to which the giver was accustomed, meaning constant pressure to produce a better product at a better price than one's competitor. The idea became accepted that a missionary should be under the same pressure for results as a business leader. Business acronyms like

ROI (return on investment) became common in discussions at givers' forums. At one seminar, I actually heard a giver speak of "more baptisms per dollar" in comparing two ministries working in South Asia. Variations of such thinking became common in giving circles. Their basic approach was to achieve their objectives by asking the right questions and seeking the right results. Shouldn't that encourage mission organizations to work smarter and to improve financial practices?

The message was loud and clear: providing statistics and some semblance of evaluation strategies could earn a mission a better shot at a grant. It seemed institutional givers valued comparative "efficiency" over specific effectiveness. If for the same money you could save one hundred souls with Mission A while Mission B was saving one soul, wasn't it wiser—and a better stewardship of God's resources—to fund A rather than B?

It took me a while to penetrate the fog of this reasoning that was sweeping through giving circles as the Era of Outcomes took root. Several observations helped to clear my thinking.

It should have been no surprise—nor should it be now—to discover that many Christian nonprofits aren't run optimally. You have only to look at my own story. I was in way over my head when I first started at the Rescue Mission. I have learned since that I wasn't the only one who, when starting in God's work, felt like I was thrown into the deep end of a pool and was expected to keep my head above water. This feeling of inadequacy and need for dependence on God is often present when believers get together anywhere in the world, for the sake of God's kingdom, to solve some challenge that needs righting in their community—whether it is helping people understand that there is a God and He loves them or solving some social ill.

They get started because they're passionate about the transformation they want to see occur and they are not necessarily focused on all the transactional, everyday responsibilities of management and spending money efficiently. Most of the new autochthonous leaders I've encountered—pastors, elders, or volunteers from local churches as well as those from the private sector—more often than not, have had no training in management or in fundraising. Using money efficiently isn't their focus. *Finding it is.*

Moreover, the pressures on a mission penetrating the darkness with the gospel are in a vastly different realm than the typical competitive pressures faced in the business arena. The places in the world where the gospel hasn't been preached are among some of the most difficult working environments on earth, where life is often a mean existence with injustice and grinding poverty as the norms, and cultural barriers to the life-saving message of Jesus are entrenched.

For some of these autochthonous missions, just launching out is a supreme act of courage. Leaders in these settings face not only their own proclivity to error and failure, which is common to all human enterprise, but they also face our common enemy, Satan—the same foe whose strategy against humanity has proven so successful, beginning in the garden of Eden. This mortal enemy, using people he has deceived, will martyr mission workers if given the chance. If he can't do that, he'll hamper them at every opportunity. And if that falls short, he'll help mission workers succeed at the wrong thing—which may suit his purposes even better, as he gets them to do his work for him while thinking they're working for God.

Sorting this all out is the tough work of mission leadership. Thankfully, we have the Holy Spirit, plus wise counsel of the elders in our community. They help us distinguish lies from the truth and merely good ideas from those that are truly God-ordained. We just need to follow the rubric that all of God's ideas are good ones, for He is good, but not all apparently "good" or "successful" ideas are led of Him. That's why accountability is so important. Any of us can get this wrong, even with the best intentions.

As for the giver's search for return on investment in missions, I came to see the error in the idea that saving one soul is somehow less valuable than saving several. A couple of Scripture passages stand out to me. There's the apostle Peter's description of the Lord as "not wanting anyone to perish, but everyone to come to repentance" (2 Peter 3:9). The same message comes through especially in the famous story Jesus told:

> Suppose one of you has a hundred sheep and loses one of them. Doesn't he leave the ninety-nine in the open country and go after the lost sheep until he finds it? And when he finds it, he joyfully puts it on his shoulders and goes home. Then he calls his friends and neighbors together and says, 'Rejoice with me; I have found my lost sheep.' I tell you that in the same way there will be more rejoicing in heaven over one sinner who repents than over ninety-nine righteous persons who do not need to repent. (Luke 15:3–7)

In business, it's sometimes said that the first sale is the hardest. Perhaps that's also true about the first convert in a mission's work. The pioneer missionary who leads only one to faith is being just as faithful to his or her particular call from God as the missionary gathering an abundant harvest after others have "planted" and "watered" (1 Cor. 3:7). There may be a vast difference in cost between the work of planting a ministry and the later work of harvesting. But both are important, and you can't do one without the other.

Nonetheless, as statistics began to rule the day in the Era of Outcomes, the idea became prominent that more numbers beget more money.

BEING EFFECTIVE

This numbers-to-money equation was a false equivalence. It meant that we in the West became inundated with statistics-centered reports of huge strides being made by church planters. A whole new industry of mission consultancy was born just to survey gospel opportunity. The 10/40 Window—the area on the global map between the physical latitudes of 10 and 40, where most of the unreached peoples of the earth reside—captured many imaginations, not only as a descriptor of where the gospel hadn't penetrated but as a strategic rallying cry for allocating resources. With the right application of business pragmatism and asset distribution, couldn't we complete the task of preaching the gospel to the whole world? This powerful idea attracted a considerable amount of money and brought distant vistas of neglected populations into the mission mainstream, particularly for Western givers. The rush to numbers obscured the difficult work being undertaken by missionaries to go where no one had preached before, and who began their journey with only a trickle of success and a flood of promise.

Numbers thinking also brought into focus suspicion that outcomes were being padded. This in turn seemed to provoke an outbreak of cynical distrust. People within international granting circles and respected leaders and elders from the majority-world church noticed a murky veil of competition creeping into the general consciousness of the missions community; it was fueled by the false idea that there is only a very limited supply of money, and that only the most efficient by measurement and not the most effective by evaluation could survive.

There was a ministry I once encountered that claimed it had reached the entirety of a large Asian nation with the gospel message, and another, more recently, that claimed it had trained nearly a million house pastors in the same region. When looking deeper, I discovered the first was claiming complete gospel penetration of the nation because it had distributed a number of gospel pamphlets equal to the number of households, and the other based its claim on the number of individuals that had signed up to view a gospel broadcast on television and had agreed to invite their neighbors to join them. There was a lot of money chasing after these phenomenal statistics, but evidence of fruit was elusive.

On the other hand, I have noticed that money is almost always tight for those who do impactful work. And it's not because God's hand is short. Their cash crunch almost always derives from the fact that effective ministries spend all the money they get to do even more ministry.

During the years after Western missionaries were expelled from China in the early '50s, the gospel continued to spread, in part, through what was known as the Bible Women.[1] Uncounted numbers of these women served as itinerant evangelists who walked the villages of the rural countryside and climbed the stairs of urban apartment houses to preach the gospel. I had the privilege of meeting one of the last of these women some years ago. At the time, she was in her 80s, and she was still walking the rural villages and climbing innumerable stairways. She had holes in her sneakers. I asked the person that introduced us if I could at least give her what cash I had in my pocket so she could buy new shoes. He told me, "She'll just spend it on more tapes and pick another pair of shoes out of somebody's trash pile."

This woman is an example of efficiency and effectiveness. I don't know how to number the uncounted people who owe their walk in Christ to her persistent walking to find them. Neither she, nor our mutual friend, asked me for money for their ministry. Though we had been introduced by someone both of us trusted, we had not yet entered into a relationship of trust and accountability.

I find you need trust to operate effectively. And in the Outcomes Era, suspicion of padded statistics, occasionally backed up with factual exposure, meant trust went out the window. The suspicion was driving the emerging fear that fraudulent financial practices were at play. Aggravating this perception was a broad lack of precise understanding about mission finance factors. This was something I was made aware of in the mid-1980s while serving on the standards committee of the Evangelical Council of Financial Accountability (ECFA).

The ECFA was formed in 1979 by recognized elders of the American missions movements—people like Rev. Billy Graham, Bill Bright of Campus Crusade, and Stan Mooneyham of World Vision. It was organized to head off government intervention at a time of increasing public concern over questionable fundraising practices among nonprofit agencies.

My experience with the ECFA was as educational as anything a nascent grant-maker could wish for. The standards committee was tasked with reviewing applications for certification. It was our job to chase down problems and to clear up any concerns of fraudulent practices. We reviewed certified audits and financials that were required of ministries to gain certification. Led by a federal judge and the finest financial, legal, and accountancy professionals from the evangelical community, it was a formidable panel to serve on. I was the token donor representative—completely out of my league.

I faced confusion particularly in regard to assessing appropriate levels of administrative and fundraising costs for a mission organization. There's a persistent belief in mission-granting circles that such costs should be kept within a fixed percentage of a mission's budget; some put the proper figure at 5 percent, others at 10 percent, and others as much as 25 percent. Everyone involved—both major givers as well as mission leaders—seemed to have some internal benchmark they held to. I never did. Having led a mission with no business or management background, I just paid the bills and tried to allocate our limited money where it would be most effective. In earlier years I got away with this rather loose practice, but when reading proposals and trying to make sense of the mission budgets I was being asked to judge, the issue became more complex.

Even members of the ECFA committee—some of the finest financial minds in Christendom—couldn't agree on what was an appropriate percentage of money to spend on fundraising and overhead. Every organization we reviewed required a nuanced understanding of program expenses versus administration and fundraising costs.

A startup ministry, for example, might have much higher fundraising costs while it established a donor base. Another problem was that home office expenses such as secretarial support, rent, and newsletter printing and mailing were typically seen as administrative costs, yet similar expenses for their offices "in the field" were viewed as program costs. And how should an overworked mission executive account for his or her time when a typical hour might include ten minutes talking to a donor (clearly a fundraising expense), twenty minutes reviewing the expense budget with the bookkeeper (clearly administrative), and thirty minutes on a phone call with a missionary in the field (clearly a program cost). Is a mission executive supposed to keep a time sheet like an attorney?

Sorting this out was mindboggling—and important, because key donors' decisions seemed to rest on a mission's ability to keep administrative costs low.

And all this begged the nagging concern over questionable fundraising practices, which had triggered ECFA's founding in the first place.[2] In reviewing audits, ECFA's standards committee found quite a few organizations wanting, but committee members used their well-developed judgment to penetrate the haze of each set of financials. For the most part, we found that applicants were in compliance, but every now and then something didn't pass what these respected men and women called the "Smell Test." Sometimes everything seemed to line up correctly in a set of audited books, but committee members still suspected that something wasn't quite right. Only rarely was actual fraud detected. Most of the time, after further investigation, it was just sloppy practices that were at fault.

In my own thinking, I began to view a mission organization's *entire* budget as administrative. After all, the money went to purchase stuff—food, blankets, drill rigs, plane tickets, whatever—to pay the rent and to cover the needs of workers, whether they were field missionaries raising their own funds or an administrative assistant on salary in the home office. What became important to me was their *effectiveness*—the presence of fruit and faithfulness and sacrifice in their ministry. It wasn't their efficiency; nor, more importantly, was it anything like "baptisms per dollar."

If It Isn't Easy, That's Normal

Others like me who looked closely at this issue of efficiency versus effectiveness could see that the typical ministry could be run more efficiently and its resources be better allocated; but we didn't assume that the vast majority of them were not on the up and up. Still, the fear that something was amiss persisted.

Those of us who traveled not only encountered actions and ministries that inspired us, but sometimes we witnessed incidents that confirmed our suspicions. On one of my early trips to India, accompanying my friend and mentor, Phill Butler, we visited a "reading room" ministry in Bombay (now Mumbai). The ministry site—supposedly designed as a place where non-literate slum-dwellers could come to hear the daily newspaper read to them followed by a Bible reading—turned out to be a walled compound next to India's largest slum. As we pulled up, we met a heavily chained gate with two large guard dogs blocking our way. Once we were granted admission, we were ushered into the designated reading room. We were overwhelmed by the smell of new paint. The shelves lining the wall were lacking any appropriate or viable reading materials.

While we were served tea by a none-too-friendly woman, I peeked behind some drawn curtains. Before me was an ante-room haphazardly stacked with the kind of furniture one would find in a prosperous home. We quickly realized these things had been cleared away from the larger area to create the illusion of an actual reading room.

I learned later that this was the home of the brother of the Indian leader who'd raised the funds for the reading room. Our visit had caught them by surprise; or perhaps we'd run smack into the middle of a family fundraising business disguised as a mission.

Later that afternoon, on our second site visit of the day, we entered the studio of a ministry that purported to have an exclusive contract to air Christian films on the government-controlled national TV network. Once again, we were overwhelmed by the smell of new paint as we were ushered into a room where an expensive dubbing machine sat on a pedestal like a statue under a spotlight. The machine had been funded to dub English-language Christian films into the network's twenty-nine broadcast languages. The real situation soon exposed itself. This costly machine wasn't being used because they hadn't found anyone to operate it. Moreover, the broadcast rights they claimed to own were somewhat suspect, or at least overblown; so was the connection to the TV network. On top of that, I came to understand that this ministry, instead of creating its own studio, could have used one of the many already in place for serving India's Bollywood movie industry.

Experiences like these taught me to ask better questions as a grant-maker in my attempt to find good ministries to fund in the successful and sacrificial Indian missions movement that was gaining steam at the time.

For me and many of my colleagues who were also trying to understand funding in India, it was a confusing time.

Another lesson I learned happened during a trip to Europe to explore grant-making opportunities. This was in the mid-1980s, and one of my first trips; I was still new at my job and full of questions.

I was an American attending a conference of European mission leaders who, to me, seemed hostile; they probably weren't, but I'm sure my persistent questions didn't inspire them to roll out the welcome mat. I'd been a newspaperman, and when I didn't know the answer to something, my habit was to ask questions until I figured it out. But as a newly minted philanthropist at a conference with seasoned missionaries from Europe, I was out of my element.

Finally, a delegate from a northern European country had had enough of my line of questions. I don't remember what I'd been asking at the time, but I do remember what happened next.

A nearby woman had been listening to my question-filled conversation with someone; suddenly she stepped right under my face. Seething with displeasure, she said, "You bloody Americans! Why don't you just send your money and shut up?" She said it with such a hiss that spittle flew out of her mouth. I didn't have a rejoinder, then or now. I just remember wondering, "Why would anyone give money after being told to shut up?"

No one but a fool wants to be loved for their money, and it felt like she believed, because the cause of the ministry I was looking into was righteous, the ministry was entitled to my employer's funds. Or maybe her outburst sprang from a deep pit of hurt by boorish Americans who may have come before me. No matter the source of her sentiment, the problem is thinking of fundraising as merely a transaction and nothing more.

To the fundraiser trapped in this thinking, getting money is the focal point. You might say the European leader represented the far end of the transactional spectrum of fundraising—where givers are objectified, as if they really are nothing more than a wallet in the bride of Christ.

HONORING THE BRIDE

As mentioned, givers can act boorish, and sometimes ministries that need money can be dismissive of the people giving it, seeing them only as useful as the money they give.

I've been guilty of this.

Forty years ago when I started working at the Rescue Mission, I took on the task of finding the money for our work. I put together a slide show and began sharing it in churches that were taking notice of the alarming increase of homelessness that co-incided with the closing of state mental hospitals and the end of the Vietnam War. Our Mission was small but highly impactful. We fed and housed hundreds of people every week with very little money.

In preparing my presentation, I hit upon the idea that we, the Mission, were the arm of the church serving the least, the last, and the lost. The poor and homeless needed help, and we needed money to help them. We were serving as an extension of the church reaching out to them; therefore, we *deserved* the church's money—so my thinking went. I was a new Christian, full of ideas that weren't necessarily biblical or spiritually formed.

So when I spoke in these churches, I always wanted an offering to be taken. That was my singular focus. I almost literally said to church members, "You don't have to get your hands dirty. We'll do it for you." I felt righteous in my message.

I was popular with church secretaries at the time, because along with my presentation for the Mission, I gave them a tangible way to deal with homeless persons who frequently came into their office begging for food or money (usually with a well-rehearsed story of a grandmother they needed to see before she died, and all they needed was bus fare to visit her one last time). I gave the secretaries a stack of coupons for admission to the Mission. I also instructed them to keep a stack of $5 bills in their petty cash so that when someone came in and begged, they could offer the coupon, call a cab, pay for it, and send the beggar to us.

I spoke to dozens of churches, taking up what amounted to small offerings that, with our meager mailing list, barely kept the Mission afloat. I was so bad at fundraising, Lewis and I had to often forgo salaries, while we and our guests were sustained by an abundance of donated day-old donuts and weak coffee.

Then, two Sunday nights in a row, in two separate churches, a special offering was taken for the Mission but was never passed along to us. As you can expect, my first reaction was anger. I considered the pastors of those churches to be thieves. *That was God's money! What were they thinking?*

God didn't let me stew in my anger for long. During a night of tossing and turning in my bed, playing out all sorts of imagined conversations with these pastors, I was visited with a thought that I'm convinced came from God. Filtered through my own language, the essence was this: "Stop objectifying my bride, whom I love."

Chastised and contrite, I realized the pure unvarnished truth of the command. I'd been seeing the church only for the money it had—not as the bride of Christ. Not to be served, but to serve my purposes, which I could justify as godly. It was where the money was, which was the only reason I had stepped through their doors.

I immediately changed my approach. First, in all churches where I spoke thereafter, I told them *not* to take up an offering for the Mission, but instead to be prepared to become part of the solution. On our Mission's brochure, I added these words in red block letters: "If you feel led to give to the Rescue Mission, please give only over and above your normal giving to your church."

I also completely changed my presentation. Drawing from the parables of Matthew 25, I began focusing on the mutual responsibility of the church and the Rescue Mission to the homeless and poor of Orange County where we lived and worshiped.

When I preached, it was simple. I had moved past the sole transactional approach to the essence of the transformation we were seeking for the homeless of our community.

The response was overwhelming. Funding for the Mission—even though churches were no longer taking special offerings for us—increased by a factor of four in the first year of my personal reformation. Moreover, every time I spoke, people came forward and pressed into my hand their business cards or notes with their address, often saying something like, "I've been waiting to hear this."

Without my planning it, the message had become a catalyst to spark vision in churches. Everyone with eyes to see had observed the rise of homelessness and the increasing number of bag ladies in our county. Now they knew how they could respond—and it was about more than money.

In every setting, there were a few whose vision began to gain clarity. And in this, there was another lesson for me. Before, if I spoke to a hundred people, I thought success was winning over the majority of my audience to what I was pitching. After my reformation, I began realizing that God was constantly preparing His people—*His bride*—to see all the needs around them, and He was calling a few out of the hundred to meet the need we were addressing. So if, as a result of my presentation, only three persons chose to come alongside us on our journey, that to me was overwhelming success. I began looking for those few that God had chosen to get involved—those who'd developed a vision and who felt a tug to share our calling and purpose.

We began getting so many volunteers, I had to hire a coordinator to help churches organize their urban teams. We started a program called Operation Love that encouraged small groups in churches to partner with Meals on Wheels, an outreach to elderly shut-ins, to fix up their homes. This ministry turned out to be providential for me as I met my wife on the first Operation Love outreach.

Not only did I meet my wife because of my changed approach, the Mission gained a measure of predictability to our funding and we were able to greatly expand our reach into the community, all through the power of true partnership.

It turns out the lesson I learned then helped me later to confront a new challenge when I was tasked with forming a committee to create what became known as the Lausanne Standards.[3]

As the twenty-first century dawned, the overall picture in worldwide mission funding was disrupted by the emergence of the ownership and engagement paradigm. Facing suspicions of fraud, concerns over inefficiency, and the objectification of donors and missions alike, it felt to me, as I immersed myself in the arcane of the issue, that granting had spiraled into a chaotic series of unfortunate encounters. Belief-defying statistics flew around like debris in a fierce windstorm.

For those of us active in grant-making back then, it's no overstatement to say that distrust began to rule the day. It was the committee's observation that givers wanted more accountability and were unwilling to offer trust. Competition for donor attention and dollars bred jealousy and rancor in the harvest fields. And the changing dynamics of our funding paradigms brought new tensions and conflict.

Authentic missions were still producing real fruit for God's kingdom through sacrificial faithfulness to their callings, but the

threat appeared real of their being overrun by rampant suspicion, fear, exaggerations, and culture clashes.

Was there an answer?

Duh!

Like everything else of eternal importance, the answer
is found in Scripture—where "the main things are the plain
things," as my pastor of many years ago John Wimber was fond of
saying. As I pondered what's really plain in Scripture, of course, I
kept landing on the truth that love can't be bought.

And this has deep significance for God-honoring fund development and organizational development.

Jesus says that His followers will be known by our love (John
13:34–35), but across the global scope of evangelicalism, failure
to love is common, especially as we encounter racial, cultural,
and doctrinal differences among us. We may assume such things
are of little consequence, but in reality, they easily create deep
suspicion and division.

Scripture shows us that God has bound us so closely
together (as Paul insists) that not one of us can ever say to another, "I don't need you"; God has designed the body of Christ
"so that there should be no division in the body, but that its parts
should have equal concern for each other" (1 Cor. 12:21–25).

Paul goes on to show us in the thirteenth chapter of 1 Corinthians that it is love that closes the differences between us and
covers the sin that disrupts our communion.

These are good words, but what were we to do about it?

In 2007, a task force commissioned by the Lausanne Committee for World Evangelization and drawn from a variety of backgrounds and cultures, launched a world-wide research project to

bring the disrupting forces to light and suggest standards to help prevent further recurrences. A process of study and reflection was undertaken over a three-year period, which led to the introduction of the standards at the third Lausanne Congress of Evangelization, held in Cape Town, South Africa, in 2010.

The work to create the standards began innocuously enough at a conference at the Oxford Center for Mission Studies. For two and a half days, donors from the West met with church elders and ministry leaders from the majority world to formulate a plan to deal with the mounting problems being observed. A book could be written on what happened next, but at the end of the conference, I found myself—quite unwilling at first—appointed as a Lausanne senior associate, tasked by First Fruit and Lausanne to form a committee to search out the issue and suggest solutions.

The task force began the process with an extensive worldwide survey and ended with a simple call for a dialogue based on a few simple standards.[4] They are as follows:

- Respect each other as fellow stewards of the gifts given to each of us as signs of the arriving kingdom of God. (Rom. 12:3, 10)
- Honor and embrace God-given cultural differences, finding strength in them as interdependent members of the body of Christ, dependent together on God. (Eph. 2:19–22)
- Communicate effectively with integrity, together discovering the Lord's vision for our common task. (James 3:17–18)

- Learn from each other, growing in flexibility, maturity, and unity in Christ as we listen to him together and watch him at work in our partnership. (1 Cor. 12:18–21)
- Learn to trust God and each other, and at the same time to be accountable to God and to each other, taking care to understand trust and accountability within each other's cultural context. (2 Cor. 5:9–11)
- When we do these things, especially across differences of culture and material wealth, we can hope to demonstrate the transforming, unifying power of the Holy Spirit, glorifying God's name among the nations through our lives and deeds. (1 Peter 2:9–12)

In the chapters that follow, we will explore the outworking of these affirmations and the attributes of missional people that can encourage communion and effective mission.

WHEN A TRUE COMMUNION OF GIVING AND RECEIVING EXISTS, THE GIVER OFFERS TRUST TO THE RECEIVER TO DO HIS JOB.

For when a true communion of giving and receiving exists, the giver offers trust to the receiver to do the job without looking over his shoulder. In turn, the giver receives accountability from the receiver, and can therefore be assured he has done his best before God with the resources God has given him. Each party, in the simple financial transaction between them, offers the other what they need.

When money goes on mission

... it is most effective and facilitates transformation when there is a Christ-centered relationship between the giver and the receiver. They are in communion and are equal at the foot of the cross.

Part 2

DRAWING EACH OTHER INTO COMMUNION

4

THE EAGLE AND THE FISH

The Pursuit of Faith and Excellence

I HAVE A SORT OF theological idea about fish. It is not to be found in Scripture; nonetheless, my idea helps me understand why I get skunked (a technical term for not catching anything) most of the time when I go fishing. I am sure this has nothing to do with a lack of ability but everything to do with the fish's refusal to submit to its God-given purpose. I believe it is the glory of the fish to be caught and eaten. I take this idea loosely from the promises in Scripture about God's provision for the birds and for us. However, it's clear from all the fish I have encountered that they do not agree and do all they can to escape me, my lures, and my imitation flies. They are, it seems, mostly unimpressed with my camouflaged waders and my stealthy behavior.

Eagles get skunked too. There are two breeding pairs that hang out near our home here where I live on Whidbey Island's Useless Bay, Washington and I am sure if we could have a conversation about this, they would agree with me that the fish are not cooperating with their God-given purpose. For the eagle, this is a matter of life and death. For me, it's much less so. After all, I can still go to the market and buy a fish that someone else has caught. This is a definite advantage.

Eagles spend long hours most days fishing. They start by perching on high branches of Douglas firs on the edge of the bluff observing the water below and waiting for an opportunity to strike. Often, they are harassed by much smaller birds that fly darting aerial maneuvers around them making sure the eagles know they are not welcome in the neighborhood. Ignoring their harassers, when an eagle judges the time is right, it soars high above the bay in big slow circles until it spots a fish that has dared to come close to the surface. The eagle then swoops down in a magnificent dive, plunging into the water with great violence, its talons extended in a mesmerizing display of dominance personified, until it surfaces, often fishless, bedraggled, and soaked to its pin feathers. The eagle does this over and over again until it gets a fish and its daily provision.

I know how the eagle feels. I've stood in bone-chilling water frozen to my armpits, casting over and over again, and unlike the eagle, I usually go home and just talk about the one that got away. Most of my friends who fish are much better at it than I am, because they have put the time in to learning the sport. I'm just a happy novice who occasionally gets lucky and catches a fish.

Fundraising is a lot like fishing that way. If you don't know your tackle (rod, reel, flies) and the water you're fishing, luck is your only friend. And from direct experience in both giving and receiving, giving is a lot like fishing as well. The more you're thoughtful about it, the better you are at it.

PRACTICE AND FAITH

When we are called to build an organization for missional

outreach or to invest in the process, what is required of us is nothing less than excellence in our practice and a full reliance on faith in God for the results . . . another paradox.

I mentioned this thought to my friend, author Henry Cloud, and he replied, "Oh, that's easy, 'Fly to where the bugs are!'" He was referencing Luke 12:24: "Consider the ravens: They do not sow or reap, they have no storeroom or barn; yet God feeds them. And how much more valuable you are than birds!"

> **WHAT IS REQUIRED OF US IS EXCELLENCE IN OUR PRACTICE AND A FULL RELIANCE ON FAITH IN GOD FOR THE RESULTS.**

Yes, God provides for the birds, but they have to work hard for their food, and they had better be good at it—just like the eagle, and frankly, just like all the rest of God's creation.

Getting God-Ordained Results

Mature Christians are well versed in the concept that faith expressed through prayer produces God-ordained results. The results may not be what we want (or thought we wanted), but our faith—worth more than gold—assures us that, as we all know, God's answers are the correct ones.

So if we're called by God to build an organization, we pray. We pray for funds, wisdom, favor, protection, and discernment. We pray for others to join in the work. And finally, we pray for results.

We also work. We organize, put policies into place, research our field, and prepare for our intervention by recruiting people to help launch our strategies. We then carefully evaluate what we've accomplished and consider what changes may need to be made in our approach. It takes a lot of effort.

Sometimes it's easy to see where our work ends and God's begins and sometimes it's not so clear. If I put an apple seed in the ground and get a tree, I won't be confused about what I did and what He did, but if I ask someone for money to help an orphan and they respond, was it God that got them to grab their wallet and give? Or was it my brilliance in laying out the argument for the gift. It's all His? Right?

How do we distinguish between what's required of us, and what things only God can do?

Steep Learning Curve

I experienced this challenge, up close and personal, when I was a newly minted Christian working at the Rescue Mission, and my efforts on behalf of the poor were often less than stellar. I was inexperienced and on a steep learning curve, but I made it even steeper by my own propensity to mess things up.

Nonetheless, ministry got done and this critical lesson about faith and excellence began to be imprinted on me. This was true because no matter how much I got in the way, I learned firsthand that God cares far more for the least, the last, and the lost than I ever could. God used whatever He had in me, and He sent a few mentors my way to teach me what I needed to know.

What I didn't know about fundraising and management at the time could fill volumes, but God didn't let me stay that way for long.

Soon after I started working at the Mission, it became clear that we weren't welcome in our location. The city leaders were mostly people of good will, but they felt we were attracting the homeless to their downtown area, which they desperately wanted to redevelop. Our rescue mission, they asserted, was in the way of progress, and the city wanted us to move out or close up.

I didn't think it would help to tell the city leaders that, like in the *Blues Brothers* movie, we were "On a mission from God." So I tried to reason with them. That didn't help either.

Opposition is opposition no matter where you are trying to push back darkness. Ours was the more benign sort; the city fathers just wanted us to go away. But our brothers and sisters across the world, when working across cultures, can and do face more considerable pressures.

In our little corner of the world, even though we were there because that's where the homeless were and the problem would be much bigger if we left, the city leaders closed the Mission down—but not before granting us a conditional use permit to build a new facility just outside the downtown area, next to the welfare department and across the street from a city park known as "Murder Central." It was a gang-infested drug emporium serving as a convenient location where battles for market share played out in deadly regularity. The homeless, when they weren't dodging bullets, lived there among the trees and bushes.

We set about building the new headquarters and shelter at the location despite being inexperienced and having little money in the bank. I was leading the project, and against all odds and advice I served as my own contractor. We didn't have a construction loan, having been advised (by a banker) that no bank would lend to us—if we defaulted on the loan, they'd be facing the public relations nightmare of seeming to be insensitive to the most desperate needs of the community where they banked. Besides that, we didn't look too much like a good risk.

We'd also forsaken any government funding (though it had been offered) because they wanted us to separate the preaching of the gospel from the outworking of Jesus' love. Besides, I believe the government should not be in the business of paying us to preach. We wanted our financial support to come from like-minded people who joined us because of a call on their lives to minister to the homeless.

> **GOD CARED MORE ABOUT MY FAITHFULNESS TO THE PROCESS AND MY ATTEMPT TO SERVE THAN THE RESULTS OF MY EFFORTS.**

The project staggered forward as we built what we could whenever we received funds. It was the dawn of my understanding of the faith and excellence paradox that I have seen played out all over the world; that is, how to keep doing ministry when everything has conspired to stop you from doing anything at all. And most importantly, I learned that God cared more about my faithfulness to the process and my attempt to serve with excellence than He did the results of my efforts.

For more than a year, we were shut down from providing active nightly service to the homeless. We began other outreaches while building the new facility as the funds came in.

We also had another problem. Our new location proved to be unpopular with a local group of activists who were trying to wrest power from the city's established leaders. They decided the city's action toward the Mission was a good rallying tool to show that the city leaders didn't really care for needy people.

It was a volatile situation. We identified with our new neighbors and wanted to be a blessing to them. We were there to help with the problems of their neighborhood, which the city fathers had ignored for far too long.

As it turned out, our intentions didn't matter. We found ourselves in a lawsuit that sought to stop our construction before we could open.

It all came to a head during a mission board meeting one late Wednesday night in the spring of 1983. It was held in a trailer I'd rented as my office on the construction site. This meeting was more contentious than any we'd ever had.

First, I reported that the construction of the Mission was all but complete; however, we were dead stopped needing several thousand dollars to finish the project.

Then our pro-bono attorney gave a dire report, warning us that because of how long the construction was taking, a superior court judge had moved up the court hearing for our opposition's lawsuit to shut us down. Our attorney told the board we had to be open and operating within fourteen days or else the judge could hand down a ruling that killed the Mission's future.

You can imagine the consternation on the part of my board. They peppered me with questions about our fundraising, centered along the lines of "Have you gone to all our previous donors and asked for further gifts?" When I countered that I'd exhausted every option I knew of, their responses bordered on exasperation.

It grew late, and everyone was weary. When it became clear we were just repeating ourselves over and over again, the quietest member of the board stood up. All eyes were turned on him. "If you ask what man can do," he said, "you get what man can do. If you ask God what He can do—you get what God can do."

Then he prayed: "Dear God, you've heard all that has gone on here tonight. We're out of answers, and we're tired and want to go home to our beds. We look to you for help. Amen."

The meeting broke up, and we left in silence.

Driving home, I felt that I had let God down. I felt helpless. Only the board knew of our situation; I didn't believe in crying wolf to donors, and I hadn't known until that night that our fate hung on the new facility being open before that court date in two weeks.

This wasn't the first time I'd been in a situation of having no idea how God was going to deliver us, and it wasn't the first time I'd lost all confidence that He would. Exhausted, I fell into a troubled night of sleep.

Early the next morning, I was startled awake by a call from the Mission secretary, who was excitedly screaming into the phone. I didn't even take time to shower as I sped back to our trailer office.

When I arrived, I found her sitting in front of a small cardboard box filled to the top with gold and silver bars and a collection of rare coins. She had arrived at the Mission early that morning in case any construction workers had shown up, and she found the box on the steps leading up to the front door of the trailer. It wasn't unusual for donations to be left there, as people were always dropping off trash bags filled with old clothes or boxes with canned goods and such. As she was unlocking the door, she tried to kick the box to the side. It was unusually heavy and didn't budge. That's when she discovered it was full of treasure.

You probably won't believe my initial reaction. Rather than praising God, I wondered if some thief had left the treasure there as a guilt offering. No kidding. I even called the police to see if someone had reported a theft of gold and silver. When told no, I quickly hung up the phone as the officer on the other end of the line began asking me, "Who are you?" For some crazy reason I couldn't believe God had done such a thing for us. As you can imagine, I got over my disbelief pretty quick.

By that afternoon, my faith soared. I sold the contents of the box for nearly $15,000. Immediately, I called out the plumbers and finish carpenters, and began the last stage of construction to allow us to get our occupancy permit.

Over the next twelve days, all but the last $1,000 that we needed came in through the mail or the front door, including a donation of fifty-five mattresses. They all had a round hole in the middle, part of a failed attempt to sell pregnant women on the idea that they could sleep on their stomachs with this wonderful invention. No expectant mothers bought them, so all the entrepreneur got out of that startup was a tax donation, and we got "holy" beds for the homeless.

Finally, it was the day before the hearing. We still needed $1,000 to pay for the installation of toilets and sinks that would allow the building inspector to issue our permit. First thing that morning, a man I'd never met walked in with a check for exactly $1,000. I called the plumbers and the building inspector, and at four o'clock that afternoon, the staff and I walked across the street to Murder Central and invited the "residents" in for a meal, an "ear banging" (their lingo, as you'll recall, for our nightly evangelistic service), and a safe night's sleep.

We got "What God Could Do."

At ten the next morning, I faced the judge with our attorney. The opposition attorney began explaining to the judge that our construction must be halted so a trial could be conducted before we were allowed to open. That's when our attorney interrupted. He told the judge—to the shock of everyone in the courtroom, including reporters from the local papers—that we were open and operating, and the judge, if he so wished, could go see for himself, because when we'd left there to come to court they were just finishing up the breakfast dishes.

The judge looked startled, then fixed his gaze on the opposition attorney and as he banged down his gavel, he exclaimed that the case against us was dismissed, declaring, "I will not be responsible for putting the homeless back on the street again."

It was over. We were in the bosom of God. No one and nothing was going to snatch this victory from us or was going to snatch the homeless from Him. Despite all that was arrayed against us, including my lack of abilities, we had flown to where the bugs were, and the homeless were going to be fed—and still are. As the board member had said, "We got what God could do."

When money goes on mission

> . . . two things are critical: our trust in God to provide and our willingness to serve in excellence, with the best we have in us.

5

FAITH

Relying on God for His Provision

LEADING BY FAITH and excellence is not a balancing act. It is a daily exercise bathed in patience and is given viability through hard work. It is both full faith and full effort.

Through our work at the Rescue Mission, we planted a seed, and God in His provision gave us a tree blossoming with the fruit of a growing ministry. A decade later, when I began working at First Fruit, my business card carried this analogy into the task of giving, the other side of fundraising.

PETER AND THE PEACH

Although I can't recall ever seeing them eat one, I know Peter Ochs and his wife Gail, coprincipals of First Fruit, love peaches.

At a board meeting some years ago, after being asked about the foundation's name, Peter answered the question with a story about a God-fearing gardener who planted a peach sapling. The gardener patiently nurtured the sapling into a mature tree, until one spring his work paid off and the buds produced big, juicy, beautiful fruit. The gardener then chose the first and most beautiful peach and offered it up to the Lord to honor Him for all the peaches He had provided on the tree.

This story was helpful, since over the years as a member of the First Fruit family, I have occasionally been asked by strangers, "So, what sort of fruit do you sell?" I normally answer by quoting the passage from Exodus 23:19: "Bring the best of the firstfruits of your soil to the house of the LORD your God."

My wife Bev is a gardener, and although I haven't tried it much, I have observed that it takes a significant knowledge of dirt, involves a fair bit of planning and sweat, yet is seemingly enjoyable. And while I love fresh produce, I have also noticed gardening requires a preternatural ability to endure delayed gratification. Somehow the wait and the work make the fruit all the sweeter. Therein is the joy of gardening.

Working in the fields of the Lord is a lot like this. Patience is a necessary virtue, and of course, giving away the first and the best requires faith that God will provide. The strength to endure comes from trust.

Like strands of DNA, patience, joy, trust, offering, and abundant harvest are embedded aspirations in the name First Fruit. Practicing these attributes and finding the pathway to translate them to the philanthropic tasks of a foundation aren't always apparent. Paul, in his first letter to the Corinthians, tells us "Love is patient." Patience is perhaps the toughest and most necessary discipline of a giver.

The pace of our times seems to demand immediate and compelling results, the very antithesis of delayed gratification—not only for gardening, but for growing organizations as well.

For me, I know that I endeavor to do my best in an

atmosphere of trust, protection, hope, and perseverance. By this I mean when I know I am truly loved and trusted, I do my best not to break that trust, and that, in turn, becomes something upon which I offer back what was given to me. Now, since I have my hands deep in the metaphoric mud, so to speak, let me observe, as I think Chauncey Gardiner did in the movie, *Being There*: you must plant in the spring to harvest in the fall. Program development—that is, creativity, planning, benchmarking, and pushing for the impact you want—is a necessary element to gain the harvest.

My very wise friend Alex Araujo, a Brazilian who served in a number of key mission leadership and coaching roles during five decades of ministry, used gardening as a metaphor of patient faith on a sweat-inducing afternoon in an upper room of an old seminary in Budapest ten years ago. He spoke during a breakout session of a Lausanne Movement senior leaders conference where I was outlining future programs of the Ministry Fundraising Network, which was then known as the Resource Mobilization Working Group.

A debate had broken out on the nature of work and faith. The question was, "With a diligent enough strategic effort, can we hasten the return of Christ?" Alex, a soft-spoken man, simply took exception to the idea that with the right inputs, God is bound to give you the outputs you seek.

This idea of right inputs getting right outputs actually doesn't sound far off center on one level. In computer speak, it's known as GIGO: Garbage In, Garbage Out. But put it in the hands of a master manipulator seeking your money and it comes out as GMGY: Give Me, Get Yours. It's an attempt to "sell" the gospel—worthy of fifteenth-century indulgences—that flies under the banner, The Prosperity Gospel. Those who promote it, in fact, promise the world and peddle a heresy.

I've never met anyone working in God's harvest who wasn't, at least initially, trying to work from a position of faith; but I have met givers and receivers on the path to communion who are bedeviled by some variation of the heresy that they are somehow responsible for what God does in producing the fruit of the ministries they lead and give to.

Money and Heresy

As I sit to write these words, I am flooded with memories of too many encounters with ministries that, in the name of Jesus, prey on the unsuspecting.

The monuments these peddlers have built for themselves can be seen all over the world and all across our airwaves. Whole movements of accountability structures such as the Evangelical Council for Financial Accountability in the US, and new movements now beginning on every continent, are at work to counteract the most abusive of their practices.

We all must be good stewards of what we have, no matter the amount of our wealth. Satan's prosperity gospel preys on the poor and vulnerable—the very people God wants us to be mindful of, to help, and to nurture. The teachers of the prosperity gospel (sometimes known as the Faith Movement) ignore Paul's warning about "people of corrupt mind . . . who think that godliness is a means to financial gain" (1 Tim. 6:5). They tell the unsuspecting that if you want something, just name it and claim it. And if you don't get it, that's your fault, because of your lack of faith.

The message in bold letters is this: the more faith you have, the more goodies you get. These teachers assert, "Of course God wants you to be successful; He's not the God of failure!"

True Measure of Faithfulness

The martyrs teach us that true, godly success is measured in faithfulness, not prosperity. Their deaths should bury this pernicious lie. When we hear the news of our brothers and sisters being beheaded for refusing to recant their Christian faith, do you think any one of them began the day of their death thinking this is what they *wanted*? Nonetheless, they couldn't deny Christ when it might have saved their lives.

THE MARTYRS TEACH US THAT TRUE, GODLY SUCCESS IS MEASURED IN FAITHFULNESS, NOT PROSPERITY. THEIR DEATHS SHOULD BURY THIS PERNICIOUS LIE.

Like Shadrach, Meshach, and Abednego, who believed God could deliver them from the fiery furnace but still asserted, "If He doesn't, we still cannot deny Him," we have a new wave of martyrs today who lack prosperity but display a strength of faith to be emulated and celebrated—and, perhaps more importantly, to be remembered. This is so that liars and thieves who wear the cloak of Christianity don't deter us from a truly godly framework from which we fund the work we've been called to do.

True faith invigorates diligence, perseverance, and

sacrifice. It is His grace that makes it all endurable in any quest for excellence.

I praise God for answered prayer. It's a lonely life without it, even when the answer isn't yes. Just because the message of faith and the role of prayer have been distorted by this heresy of the prosperity gospel, we shouldn't be discouraged in the task of funding mission work. Despite the hucksterism of our age, the light from God will always shine through when He is honored.

MISSIONS ISN'T AN ATTEMPT TO "SELL" THE GOSPEL, IT'S AN EMMAUS-ROAD JOURNEY.

Again, missions isn't an attempt to "sell" the gospel, it's an Emmaus-road journey of fellowship, learning, and being swept up with the Holy Spirit.

Easy or Hard? Two Ways to Get Where You're Headed

A few years ago, I heard two men on separate occasions draw a picture from the adventurous metaphor of sailing as having significance for mission's leadership. Those two men, both of whom I deeply admire and have learned much from, were the aforementioned Alex Araujo and Roger Parrott, president of Belhaven College. Alex presented the metaphor as a devotional topic at several conferences, while Roger used it in a plenary session of a Lausanne Movement meeting, and also as the theme of the concluding chapter in his wonderful book on management, *The Longview*.[1] At the time, Alex and Roger didn't know of each other's work.

Both men used sailing as a metaphor for leaning on God's power to get to God's destination. This simple and inspiring idea of catching the wind of the Holy Spirit to lead you on your journey worked for me on a number of fronts, especially in the framework of understanding the paradox of faith and excellence.

To properly appreciate my saying this, you should know that for my wife and me, learning to sail was an exercise in crushing disappointment and excruciating futility. I wanted to learn to sail because we'd taken up residence in a small seaside village, Dana Point, in southern California. From our vantage point, every weekend we could see little boats with white sails on the blue water darting around just off the bluff. It looked cool.

So, I found a youth association that conducted sailing lessons for all comers on Saturday mornings utilizing sabots at the harbor near our home. Have you ever been in a sabot? They're tiny boats that sort of resemble a stylized bathtub with a sail. They have a hard, uncomfortable bench seat, a centerboard to keep from going sideways, a rudder connected to a stick instead of a proper wheel, and a bunch of loose ropes. I didn't even know enough to call the stick a tiller and ropes, lines.

Not that it wasn't fun, if your idea of fun is being soaked to your skivvies in cold, polluted harbor water with far too many things going on at once that you need to master. I was determined to carry on because the romantic vision of cutting across the foamy sea was lodged too deep in my soul.

Bev didn't suffer so. When she learned that one of the lessons you needed to master to graduate from the class was to deliberately flip your boat upside down in the scummy water of the harbor so you could practice saving yourself, she quit. I dropped out a bit later after I knocked myself silly with the boom several times while looking the wrong way.

Sailing is hard—and I finally accepted the truth about

myself. If I wanted to be a sea captain, I would have to command a powerboat. No matter the size, I needed a motor to do the work for me. I no longer wanted to be at the mercy of the wind.

When at sea, you have two choices: the power has to come from inside the boat, or outside. Whether you're in a dinghy with oars or a cruiser with twin diesels, if you want to be in control, make sure the power is *in* the boat.

And therein lies a fine picture of faith.

Catching the Wind of the Spirit

Successful deep-water sailors have to be excellent at what they do. They must know as much as possible about their boat, her limits, her potential, and her rigging. They must know how to manage a crew, how to read the tides, and, most importantly, how to find the wind. Without the wind they won't get anywhere, no matter their skills and knowledge. Meanwhile, depending on the wind may lead them on a wandering course—filled with delay caused by factors they simply can't control.

Contrast that with power boaters. They can harbor the illusion that if they have a motor, gas, and a boat that doesn't leak, they can achieve their desire and get to where they are going much faster and in a more direct manner than a sailor. With a hand on the throttle and the motor roaring, they can get to places in a straight line when the desire for speed is of the essence.

And who in missions doesn't want speed when trying to alleviate endemic poverty, cure a virulent disease, or, for that matter, bring the gospel to lost souls? We assume our work needs all the power we can get. The counter-intuitive idea that sailing—rather than motoring—is the best and truest way to get to our destination seems to go against our urge for mission success.

Who wants to be at the mercy of the wind?

But for sailors, the adventure is in the journey, and in this metaphor, it's our trust in God that leads us in the right way to the destination. As sailors, we must work with the wind, jibing at times, sometimes tacking, then running when the wind is at our back—but always navigating toward the destination. We must hold fast when the storms blow and be patient when the wind is seemingly gone.

This is doing God's work God's way.

God is Jehovah Jireh; He knows our needs before we ask (Matt. 6:8). We have His promise that He's with us on a journey that requires our courage, cleverness, obedience, and reliance on others as well as on God.

To journey with the movement of the Holy Spirit in our mission "sails" is sublime. To see God at work is to watch something miraculous happen when it's beyond our means or when we have an inadequate ability to deliver. Even when we experience failure and suffering in our efforts while knowing God is still with us, we learn to understand these things as a life-transforming process. They teach us to continue finding fulfillment even in tasks we dislike.

Catching the "wind" of the Holy Spirit turns out to be our greatest motivator for pursuing excellence.

When money goes on mission

. . . sometimes our path is perceived but not always understood. We must rely on God's power and not on our own power to reach our destination.

6

EXCELLENCE THAT LEADS TO EFFECTIVE GIVING AND RECEIVING

MYANMAR, IN MY MEMORY, is a country of deep mists and mysticism.

Some years ago, while traveling there for the first time, I sat on the stoop of a backstreet hotel, bleary-eyed and jet-lagged. Trying to clear my head, I was rewarded with a sight unlike anything I had ever seen—a "conga-line" of about twenty-five Buddhist monks in their saffron robes, winding their way through the neighborhood and drumming their fingers lightly on weathered brass bowls. Apparently, they were going house to house begging a handful of rice from whomever answered.

I learned later this was a social action ritual of the monks and those who gave—collecting rice for later distribution to the poor before either the monks or their givers would eat their morning meal.

I bring this up because in any pursuit of excellence in giving and receiving we must first conquer our fears of the basic actions involved in fundraising and giving. For the neophyte, fundraising is almost always, in my experience, the fear of being seen as a beggar, and for the giver, it is the fear of being seen as a con man's mark.

The only way I know how to get over these debilitating perceptions, besides lots of practice, is to have an all-in, nothing-held-back attitude, like the eagle in its swooping dive and violent plunge into water.

No matter your role, excellence means doing your best to become fully engaged in pursuing your mission's purpose—or, for that matter, your life's purpose. This attitude is so strongly felt that it must come from deep in the heart—from a place that a pastor, John McClure, called our "knower." It's a place where our calling from God is so strongly rooted, we can't be led away from it, come what may. It's the wellspring of both true faith and our true pursuit of excellence. It's as true for a leader responsible for the growth of a mission as it is for any believer.

When Excellence Is Tested

There's one place where I've seen this "all-in" attitude in mission leadership break down more than anywhere else: in the need for money and the fundraising necessary to get it.

THERE'S ONE PLACE WHERE I'VE SEEN THE "ALL-IN" ATTITUDE IN MISSION LEADERSHIP BREAK DOWN MORE THAN ANYWHERE ELSE.

At just about every opportunity when I teach or coach about fundraising, as soon as we get past the pleasantries, introductions, and the like, I begin with the question, "Do you hate fundraising?" The usual answer is so predictable, I want to quickly get it out of the way.

Working as a grant-maker, I've even had fundraisers begin a call with me by telling me they hate fundraising. I've always thought it must be their attempt to diffuse anxiety. Nonetheless, I believe that those who say it, mean it. At some level, they appear to loathe both the idea and the practice of fundraising—or at least, a lot of what they've seen of the practice.

Not all people hate fundraising. Some go about it happily, though even they have typically observed distasteful ways in which it's sometimes carried out. But for many, perhaps most, fundraising feels like begging—like asking some stranger, friend, or relative to give you money you haven't earned. It may make you feel that asking for the money means you don't have enough faith for God to provide, or you've been stuck with the one worst job in the mission. You may think you have to fall on your sword so that others can do the real work of God.

Sometimes the dislike is more benign. You may think you're being asked to be a Christian version of that monk with a begging bowl.

Sometimes the thought of fundraising leads to an existential spiritual crisis. You may think, "Shouldn't I just be praying, and shouldn't God just be providing? Or, am I fundraising because I have a personal fear of poverty?"

Or maybe your resistance to fundraising is just a time-management crisis. You can't devote the necessary time to get the money for your mission because you're being pulled in too many directions.

Worry about money is never far from the center of the issue with fundraising. However, fundraising isn't the antidote for worry. Nor is excellence. Adonai is—the Lord Jesus Christ.

The lordship of Christ is something you have to know in your "knower."

I have to admit, however, that I don't mind hearing how people hate what they've seen or experienced in fundraising. It gives me a great starting point for getting into what's really critical about understanding the task and process.

What's critical is this: *true fundraising is true leadership*. Done in true excellence and true faith, it's knowing where you're headed, and finding those who want to join you on the journey. A genuine commitment to excellence will ensure that putting such leadership into practice will be a fulfilling experience rather than a loathsome one.

Biblical Fundraising

To lead well in fundraising—with both faith and excellence—it's good to keep in mind how much fundraising we see in the Bible, and how well it's done.

We have a great example of Old Testament fundraising in 1 Chronicles 29. David gave his own wealth to build the temple, and he challenged those in his kingdom to join him as well in giving. As a result, so much was raised that they had to stop the offering.

It's also good to remember that Jesus Himself was supported by fundraising. And yes, I know, Judas carried the team purse, but that doesn't change the spirit of what was being done. Jesus didn't need the money. All you need to do is remember how He fed the 5,000 and paid His taxes (Matt. 14:13–21, 17:24–27). In Luke 8 we read about a number of women coming alongside Jesus and His disciples: "These women were helping to support

them out of their own means" (8:3). The women were expressing worship through their giving and clearly Jesus wanted them
to have the experience.

The apostle Paul, at one point in his ministry, chose to raise
funds for the benefit of fellow believers. We see him as more of
a self-supporting missionary who was helped by his friends and
who for stretches of time worked at tent-making to support his
preaching. But Paul spent a year of his life taking up an offering
among Greeks and Macedonians who were new converts and
poor, but who gave generously to aid afflicted Jewish believers
in Jerusalem. From a careful study of that offering—not only in
2 Corinthians 8–9, where Paul laid out his plans, but elsewhere
in the New Testament (Rom. 15:25–29; 1 Cor. 16:1–4; Acts
21:17; Gal. 2:9–10)—we see dynamic principles for the giving
and receiving of God's provision in God's way. Here we can really
see that Scripture offers us the best possible way to fundraise.

John Stott, when leading a group of American donors
through a study of those two chapters in Corinthians, said this:
"It is amazing to me that so much doctrine and ethics can be
involved in what, at first sight, is just a simple, straightforward
transfer of cash from one person to another or from one group
to another."[1]

In his presentation, John Stott highlighted several principles
that bear strongly on fundraising for missions.[2] (Even if you're
quite familiar with the Scripture verses mentioned above, I hope
you'll return to those chapters repeatedly to help keep their deep
truths fresh in your thinking.) John noted, for example, how Paul
teaches us that giving is an expression of God's grace. That is the
first principle of biblical giving, and it reinforces the truth that

the other side of giving is *asking*. Paul devotes two full chapters of his letter to talk about fundraising and to directly challenge the Corinthians to give.

He's emphasizing here that givers *need* to give, and the very act of giving is itself God's gift to the giver. In fact, it has always seemed hard for me to say who needs giving the most—the investor or the entrepreneur. Both seem to need it equally, and to need each other equally.

WHEN WE AS GIVERS AND RECEIVERS ARE IN SYNC WITH GOD, WE MEET AT THE FOOT OF THE CROSS IN A TRUE COMMUNION.

Paul emphasizes also that giving is inspired by Christ's incarnation and life and death: "For you know the grace of our Lord Jesus Christ," he writes, "that though he was rich, yet for your sake he became poor, so that you through his poverty might become rich" (2 Cor. 8:9). Giving is inspired by the example we have of Christ leaving the wealth and beauty of heaven, sacrificing all that He had and all that He was for us. When we as givers and receivers are in sync with God, we meet at the foot of the cross in a true communion.

In emphasizing another clear principle in this passage, Paul asserts that giving should be proportionate to our wealth: "according to your means," he says. "For if the willingness is there, the gift is acceptable according to what one has, not according to what one does not have" (8:11–12). God wants us to willingly give what we have, not what we don't have. So, it's *proportional* giving, proportionate to our wealth. This is where the prosperity heresy is especially exposed for the fraud that it is. We are not to give what we don't have.

Paul, tellingly, also emphasized the need for careful supervision for large-scale gifts. Paul appointed his top people and dedicated them to the offering project, which took a year to accomplish. Paul offered accountability to these donors: "We want to avoid any criticism of the way we administer this liberal gift. For we are taking pains to do what is right, not only in the eyes of the Lord but also in the eyes of man" (8:20–21). This is true communion, allowing givers to experience the joy of what the gift accomplishes. And in return for such accountability, givers offer trust.

Such giving pleases and honors God especially by turning hearts toward Him in gratitude. Paul says that such generosity "is not only supplying the needs of the Lord's people but is also overflowing in many expressions of thanks to God" (9:12). When the loving actions of the gospel are accomplished because of the actions of the giver and receiver—both the missional investor and the entrepreneur—then joyful thanksgiving abounds in many directions, and people experience the true meaning of the gospel.

Marks of Excellence

In pursuing excellence and faith, we take to heart these incredible biblical principles related to fundraising, allowing them to build up our confidence and to carry out our mission's calling with an all-in attitude. These truths promote confidence because they stretch our faith in God, whose Spirit inspired Paul to record those fundraising principles.

Just as in learning to sail, there are key attributes we must have and develop to be effective in ministry—to demonstrate excellence. Recognizing and understanding these attributes are helpful both for the giver and the mission leader. It builds up motivation for givers as they recognize these qualities in mission leaders, just as it motivates leaders to pursue excellence in each area.

So, what are these key attributes? How do they mark the mission leaders who'll catch the wind of the Spirit—and whose work will most compellingly motivate people to give? I've observed that the following factors represent the most important criteria:

- They demonstrate godly *leadership*.
- They communicate their mission's *purpose* and *ideas* for going forward in a way that creates a communion of giving and receiving among missional entrepreneurs and missional investors.
- They possess good *character*.
- They have a good *track record* of past ministry.

All these factors are critical for bringing partners and fellow sojourners on board to join you on your journey.

When money goes on mission

. . . an "all-in" attitude and commitment to excellence is necessary.

Part 3

LEADERSHIP AND MONEY

7

TRUSTWORTHY LEADERSHIP

"You Can't Lead If You Can't Follow"

MISSION PHILANTHROPY is highly focused on leadership.

Givers—both small and large donors—are stewards and not the owners of their resources. And, as such, these living stones may not always think of themselves as leaders. However, the choosing of who to invest with for the purpose of increasing the Master's profits is a form of direct leadership. It not only provides needed resources, it confers endorsement and can even help, in a true communion, to add value to how receivers go about their work.

However, fundraising should never be giver driven, which is an inappropriate use of donor leadership. Just ask yourself, "Am I doing what God called me to do or what this individual with money wants me to do?" Major givers, when meeting with ministry leaders about the possibility of making large grants, often lead with their questions, even if they don't realize it. If you want to know what givers are interested in, just pay attention to what they ask you about. Proposals, no matter how well written and presented, are an inadequate representation of ministries. Often, as a grant-maker, when I met with leaders of intriguing ministries, I was aware of their frustration with some of my questions because they were trying to guess what I would respond positively to. I asked questions to learn about them and didn't know yet, myself, if I could recommend them for funding.

Tom McCallie is the former executive director of the Maclellan Foundation, one of the largest and most influential of the evangelical philanthropies that give to overseas missions. Today, he is still making grants and is president of the Westwood Endowment. He is known for asking tough and probing questions. His questions can be intimidating when you first meet with him, but questions like his are actually an important part of the ministry of giving. Tom developed his skills in questioning as an attorney. A good question, he asserts, seeks to understand what's really going on in ministries that may not be represented in their proposals. His questions actually might be more helpful, in a strange way, than money. I'm not sure everyone would agree with this sentiment, but it does happen when an investor's questions help you see an opportunity you didn't think you could reach for, or a blind spot you didn't know you had. Or they can help you bring clarity to the narrative of your work.

WHO MINISTRY LEADERS *ARE* IS A FAR BETTER PREDICTOR OF SUCCESSFUL, GOD-DEFINED OUTCOMES THAN WHAT THEY *DO*.

However, investors, both large and small, know that if you want to get something done for widows and orphans, for the oppressed, for the physically and spiritually needy, you'll need a mission, and that mission will need a prepared leader.

The problem is that, most often, the focus is on what ministry leaders do, not who they *are*. And who they are is a far better predictor of successful, God-defined outcomes.

FOLLOWING TO LEAD

On my first day of work at the Orange County Rescue Mission, a young former gang leader confronted me. He'd been saved and discipled by Rev. Lewis Whitehead, and he feared I was stepping in to try to take control of the Mission. After all, I was white (unlike Lewis), and I came from the dominant culture of a community that hadn't yet fully embraced Lewis.

This former gang leader's words to me, delivered with a handshake that was more warning than welcome, were these: "*You can't lead if you can't follow*." That sentence still echoes in my mind. Back then I thought that was pretty good theology, and I still do. Following to lead is counterintuitive. Jesus set the example, of course, when he prayed to the Father, "Not as I will, but as you will" (Matt. 26:39).

There's only one irreplaceable leader—Jesus Christ, our Redeemer. In His greatest example to us of His leadership, He emptied Himself of His power and took up the cross. In doing so, He accomplished His earthly mission and saved those who would call on His name. And in doing so, He showed us how to use the power invested in those who lead; that is, anyone who has followers.

If you're on top of the organization chart, your job is to make sure everyone else in the organization can do his or her job. You

ask God for direction, and you set the course. You recruit the resources and the people, and you cajole, disciple, and encourage
those God has entrusted to you to accomplish the calling He has
placed on you and on them.

Jesus did all these things with His disciples, and He washed
their feet. He also trusted them to do the work He'd given them.
He didn't micromanage or operate from a strongman model.

The Quickest Way to Kill a Grant

One time, while on a site-visit for my foundation, I visited a
once-prominent organization that had fallen on hard times and
was attempting to make a comeback. The autochthonous leader
had attracted the interest of American givers, and I decided on
an extended stay to get a good look into his work before recommending the sizable investment he was seeking. I used to call
this approach, "Wearing out my welcome." And in this case, I
definitely did.

As we walked the grounds of the ministry, I couldn't help
noticing that where gardens had been, there were now just
weeds. The buildings also showed an alarming lack of maintenance; some looked as if they'd soon crumble into complete
uselessness.

I set aside my initial concerns and wondered if this disrepair
was a legacy of the previous administration. I didn't want to
place too much importance on my first impression in a site visit.
I've come to understand that although first impressions are often
valuable, they can get you in a lot of trouble when approaching a
situation in a different culture. You think you know what's going
on when you really don't.

But this time, my visit kept going downhill. When we went inside offices, the staff snapped to attention as we entered. My concerns were further deepened as we sat down for our first meeting with key staff. Each one seemed unusually quiet and focused on the leader, who worked to keep all the attention on himself.

It was evidence of a problem I occasionally encountered when grant-making. It's the belief that the leader must control everything a potential giver sees or hears. That's why I developed a "wear out my welcome" strategy for visiting a ministry as a potential investor. By my third day there, I'd be a bother, and everyone would get back to work—which is the precise moment when you get your best insights into how things operate.

At this organization, things got worse over the next three days. Finally, on my last day there, I was walking the grounds when a family member of the mission leader chased me down, yelling, "You tell him to stay here! He's spending all his time in the United States, and this place is falling apart. He needs to be here."

As I talked with her, I learned her rage was actually fear. Fear for the ministry. Fear for her loved one. And fear that God had moved His blessing on. Because I represented an American foundation, she hoped I could force him to spend the time necessary at the organization to turn the situation around. I just nodded and mentioned that I'd speak with him.

The next day, I told him what had happened. I also informed him I wouldn't be recommending an investment in the ministry. During our conversation, he confirmed my impressions of the state of the ministry, and said he knew he was spending too much time on the wrong things.

He was then—and is now—a good man. In fact, it seems, he has subsequently turned the situation around at his mission. But on that day, he had to admit he was trapped in the model of leadership he'd inherited from the former leader, along with the legacy of the ministry. It was a micromanagement, strongman approach—sometimes known as a client-patron relationship; at its worst, it's exploitive and paternalistic. It's a dominant model of leadership that requires everyone in the organization to focus on the leader and the favors that can be dispensed or withdrawn by that leader. As the patron at the center of everything (and who keeps telling himself, "After all, God called me to this ministry, didn't He?"), such a leader is continually tempted to tighten control over the mission and even over the board. This approach attempts to ensure that the leader is central to all tasks, and therefore irreplaceable.

This is why he spent so much time in the United States raising what little money he could. He wasn't accountable to anyone giving direction to him about how he should lead.

The Value of Accountability

We unequivocally know we are like the flowers of the field— here today, gone tomorrow. Even if your name is on the front door of your ministry and you're the sole breadwinner, you're not indispensable, even though you are important—as are all the people working with you in your organization.

Believing you're indispensable is *not* the most effective way to run a ministry. When you run out of favors to distribute, you'll soon be alone at the top. Yet, I've observed far too many missions that are led in this manner, almost like a small family business, where sometimes it is hard to tell who benefits more— the family or the beneficiary.

The issue comes down to a lack of accountability. The bottom line is this: *if you can't be fired from your position, you're not accountable.* Even if you have an "accountability structure," but it includes a majority of friends, family members, and employees, then you're not really accountable. Perhaps the word *accountability* exists in your organization's bylaws, but it's just window dressing, designed to keep your legal status in check and you in power.

If this statement fits you: "Nobody else around here can run this place," then however good a man or woman you are, you haven't done what's best for your ministry.

Succession planning

I know of a Westerner running a ministry in South Asia who has been there so long he is more South Asian than Western. He has developed a high-quality ministry over the years. The ministry benefits hundreds of women and children every week. He is ethical and is well thought of. He raises all the ministry's money from a well-developed network in the West.

Years have gone by, and he's much older now, but he has no known succession plan for the ministry's leadership, other than, presumably, for the board to recruit another Western missionary to take his place when he dies. I know people who've served on his board and have implored him to develop a plan for bringing local people into key leadership roles and to position them for future leadership. He hasn't done it. If he never does, the ministry could suffer to the point of collapse.

It could be that his current board agrees with him that no autochthonous leader could possibly match his funding ability or have even a ghost of a chance to keep his funding network alive. But this isn't true, and it's based on wrong assumptions.

In situations like these two examples above—one with an autochthonous leader and one with a Westerner—the failure to lead as servants, and to devolve power in order to empower others, is keeping ministries weaker than necessary, and even threatens the work's future.

THE FAILURE TO LEAD AS SERVANTS, AND TO DEVOLVE POWER IN ORDER TO EMPOWER OTHERS, IS KEEPING MINISTRIES WEAKER THAN NECESSARY.

I learned this when I met and came under the influence of John Perkins, the great American civil rights leader, evangelist, and social activist. I've known John for nearly forty years. In all the times I visited with him, I never knew him not to have someone he was mentoring glued to his hip. Over the years, these mentored individuals—both African-American, like John, and Caucasian, like me—went on to serve in various leadership positions, including running many of the projects that John himself had started. He has willingly submitted to his board, even when he hasn't necessarily agreed with them. As a result, the ministries God used John to start are flourishing. When John passes to glory, they'll continue to flourish.

When I encounter leaders, even in the humblest of circumstances, and I see them unafraid to mentor and release power to a younger leader, it often reminds me of the wry smile that crosses John's face when you capture something he has tried to get across to you.

Leading as a Servant

As you journey together with those God has brought along to help reach the destination He has set before you, your ministry's horizon will stretch far beyond your ability to do what you can on your own. And when you put yourself into a true accountability structure, you bring along people who are as invested in the outcome of the ministry as you are. That process takes sacrifice and it takes time. Above all else, it takes putting on the nature of Jesus.

Jesus has given *us* the job of building His church and ushering His bride to the heavenly marriage table (Rev. 19:6–9). I remember my pastor from many years ago, John Wimber, looking out across the congregation and saying, "Look around, folks. It doesn't get better than this—you're *it*. You're who God has chosen to use as His witnesses." I remember thinking, *"Yikes, he's right!"*

If you're called to lead a mission organization, you probably have to delegate away the things you enjoy doing the most so that somebody else does the training, somebody else does the one-on-one ministry—while you do the resourcing. That's servant leadership.

How much time does it take?

If you lead a majority-world mission and somebody else has been doing the fundraising for your organization, but they're now saying you have to be sustainable, you're going to have to get busy. You'll have to devote as much time as you can—perhaps most of your time—to raising funds to sustain your ministry. You'll have to give responsibilities to others who join in your ministry. It requires leading as a servant. Servant leadership is not easy.

As an investor in ministry, if you are contemplating how to give in a manner that helps autochthonous mission to become sustainable, you're in for some hard work as well. You will have to be thoughtful about the outworking of your gift within the culture, scope, and size of the ministry you want to support. Working together, in a communion of giving and receiving, is the best way forward for each partner, both givers and receivers, to fulfill their God-given callings and for ministries to achieve sustained interdependence.

Excellence requires practice, just like body surfing, to get the ride of your life. In the rest of this book, we will be looking at the getting and giving of trust and accountability. Mastering these principles, I've learned, is the best way to ride high and finish fine—and to avoid the hairy wipeouts!

When money goes on mission

> ... leaders who seek funds for their work and givers who seek to put money to work for the gospel are true disciples. In communion, they are able to create a divine or elegant balance of giving and receiving that in turn creates sustained interdependence.

8

PURPOSE

The Reason for Giving and Receiving

REVEREND LEWIS WHITEHEAD found his purpose in a derelict corner of Orange County, California, home of Disneyland and one of the most unique places on earth. Orange County embodies the American dream, a place where almost anything can happen—and does.

In the mid-twentieth century, the county's land was composed mostly of bean fields and orange groves, separated by occasional suburban developments, small cities, and two Marine air bases dating back to World War II.

There were some who dreamed of a godly future for this place. One of them was Marine Sgt. Lewis Whitehead, an admiral's steward. He and a small group from a local Christian businessmen's fellowship met at 5:30 most mornings on Saddleback Mountain at a perch where they could view a good part of the county. They prayed for revival to come to Orange County. This was before the establishment of the megachurches the county came to be known for: places like the Crystal Cathedral, Melodyland Christian Center, the original Calvary Chapel, Vineyard Christian Fellowship, Saddleback Community Church, and Mariners Church. Each would come to have multiple thousands in their congregations. Back then, this wasn't so. But Lewis and his small group of friends prayed earnestly that God would visit in a powerful way.

And He did.

One unexpected consequence of their prayers was the founding of the Orange County Rescue Mission. In the early 1970s, Lewis was nearing retirement from active duty. On his drive home from the El Toro Marine Air Station, he crossed the dry bed of the Santa Ana River on the Chapman Avenue Bridge. There he began to notice a small encampment of homeless men huddled around a fire with improvised shelters of cardboard boxes and tarp lean-tos. And God began to move Lewis to be part of the answer.

WHEN GOD GIVES VISION, HE GIVES SIGHT. AND WITH SIGHT, HE CAN SHOW YOU YOUR DESTINATION.

When God gives vision, He gives sight. And with sight, He can show you your destination.

When Lewis first saw those men, he didn't have a grand vision to establish the multimillion-dollar full-service mission for the homeless that exists today. He just saw some guys in obvious need.

A few days after first spotting them, Lewis parked his car near the bridge and made his way down to the encampment. He wasn't welcomed. He pressed on anyway and began telling them about the love Jesus had for them. He'd hardly started when one of the men jumped up and took a swing at Lewis, who, despite his size, was quite agile. He dodged the intended blow, and in his best Marine bearing, helped the man sit down and continued to engage the men in a conversation about Jesus. Later he returned with some blankets and canned food and continued to urge the men to give their hearts to Jesus.

Within a few weeks, Lewis rented an old storeroom above a shoe store on Fourth Avenue in nearby Santa Ana. He invited the men and others like them to spend the night out of the weather on the floor of the storeroom in some sleeping bags his friends had donated. Lewis's wife, Merdis, brought sandwiches she'd made. Lewis offered a devotional and began to disciple some of the men who'd become believers.

A new mission was birthed.

As God does with us all, He led Lewis through a process to understand the full vision He had for his life. First, He showed Lewis a problem—a need—that He wanted addressed. Second, He began to help Lewis understand his calling to address that need. Finally, He helped Lewis understand how he was indeed fulfilling his calling.

Lewis first prayed that God would do a great work in Orange County. He wanted to be part of whatever God was up to, which turned out to be a lot. God then showed Lewis the men under the bridge. Lewis prayed as he climbed down the hill, "Lord, what shall I do?" God had Lewis begin to evangelize them. Later, Lewis wanted to do more. God had him open a shelter with food and beds to show these men God's love for them in the here and now as well as in the hereafter. With this in place, and an informal program of discipling those who wanted the completeness of Christ in their life, Lewis began to fully understand what God had called him to do.

SEEKING YOUR PURPOSE

At one level, understanding mission is simple. There's someone or a group of people who feel compelled to do something about a problem or challenge they see, and they can't shake off their concern. You and the group you've drawn together begin your discussions with a basic question: We've got to do something about this; what can we do? As the thinking and the discussion progress, as action is contemplated, you come to a point where you launch out.

You start with a purpose, which is the reason for everything. You have a goal in mind and a destination. In the problem situation you've been shown, you'll know if change has occurred.

We see an example of this in Scripture when Paul preached the gospel in Greece. He saw a people to whom God had called him and who didn't know Jesus. He had a calling to preach the gospel and to see people won to the Lord. He knew he'd done his job when his converts displayed fruit, were baptized, were formed into churches, and were developing elders and pastors—as well as giving of their resources.

Three Questions to Ask

It could be said God led Lewis through a process of answering three questions that helped him learn his God-given purpose:

1. What is God showing me?
2. What is He telling me to do about what He's showing me?
3. How will I know I'm accomplishing what I've been told to do?

I've used these three questions countless times in my quest to understand the calling of those I've tried to help in their work. The answers to these questions—taken together and explained in a brief compelling format—tell us the vision statement of a ministry. It is at the exact place of a clear statement of purpose that offers potential investors and other partners to begin their journey with us to the destination that our purpose statement defines.

Figure 1

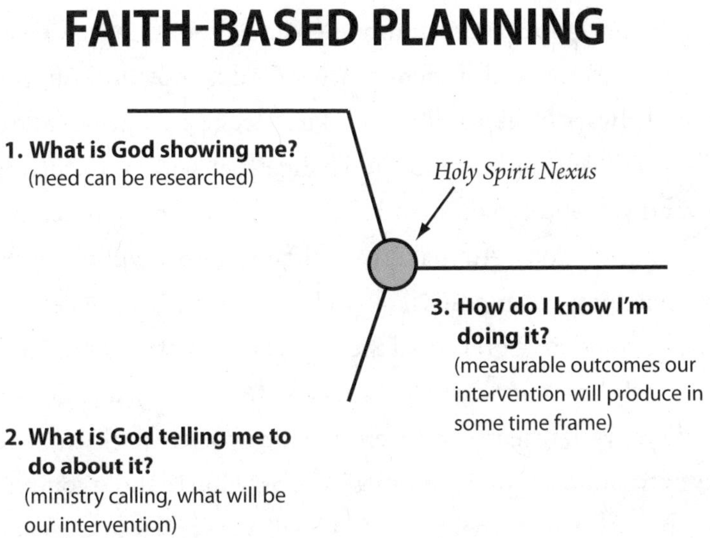

FAITH-BASED PLANNING

1. What is God showing me?
(need can be researched)

Holy Spirit Nexus

3. How do I know I'm doing it?
(measurable outcomes our intervention will produce in some time frame)

2. What is God telling me to do about it?
(ministry calling, what will be our intervention)

What Is God Showing Me?

I believe God has a call on all of us, not just leaders. He has a plan and a purpose for our lives. You may serve as a carpenter, a teacher, a parent, a business person, or as a volunteer at the local homeless shelter.

Our purpose is to serve the need He draws us toward. It's what's in focus and everything else is blurry. Like the focal plane of a camera, I believe God will give you a sharp-relief picture of the need He's drawing you to, if you ask Him for this.

Like Lewis, you may not understand it well when you first encounter it, but you will—and more importantly, you should. In time you should become an expert in the needs you're called to address. This means developing a deep familiarity through research and an incarnational depth of experience. Those who God is calling to join you on your journey will expect nothing less of you. This doesn't mean you can't in true humility express your doubts and incomprehension about things, for as a constant learner and student of what God is showing you, you should always be expanding your knowledge. If you aren't flexible, you'll misunderstand the change that will be occurring around you and the unintended consequences of your actions and interventions. An inability to adapt nimbly will mean diminished impact and missing vital junctions where necessary change could have prevented the obsolescence of your ministry. God will show you what He wants you to see. So where do you apply yourself when everywhere you look you see problems and potential ministry opportunities? You ask God to show you, and you pay attention expectantly. God will answer because He has sent the Holy Spirit for that exact purpose.

What Is God Telling Me to Do About It?
This is the toughest of the three questions to answer simply. The answer is specific to what you have seen and researched. And it

is the keystone of your purpose and what draws the giver into partnership with you.

When we first see a problem with clarity, we think of ideas of how to fix it, which itself leads to other questions. *How can I make an impact? What's being done already by others? Who else is at work, and are they effective?* These are important questions. The answers, taken cumulatively, can be important when discerning what needs to be done, but they don't answer the direct question of our calling. They are only our ideas of how we might accomplish our calling.

Here's another series of potential questions: *What is it about what I see that motivates me? Does it make me passionate? Do I sense God's voice in this? Do I sense a calling, even if it isn't defined? Do those around me sense a calling?*

What's important is to discern the essence of what needs to be done—that is, the critical key that unlocks the mystery of what really needs to happen. It's the essential insight that defines what you see.

To keep from mixing up strategy with mission and calling, what might be helpful is to continually revisit this question: *What is God telling me to do about what He's showing me?* Remember that while strategies will always change to meet changing circumstances, calling is always constant in the context. Our essential calling can most often be stated in a way that's concise, clear, and even obvious. And it's descriptive of your *destination*—not how you're going to get there. Strategies and ideas explain how you hope to achieve your purpose in your current planning.

For example, when I needed to raise funds for a vehicle for the Mission, if I had just focused on the strategy of having a truck

WHILE STRATEGIES WILL CHANGE TO MEET CHANGING CIRCUMSTANCES, CALLING IS CONSTANT IN THE CONTEXT.

pick up donated goods and groceries, it might not have helped givers understand that the truck's core purpose was to facilitate our expression of integral mission. The truck, an ordinary thing in and of itself, only made sense in how important it was to fulfill our purpose. All strategies, really, are like this. Mostly they fund ordinary things. But they come alive in the passion of the particular mission when seen in the light of that mission's purpose. Givers most readily join you in your purpose, and they fund strategies to achieve it. Strategies are in and of themselves ordinary things and activities; when seen in the context of higher purpose, they become meaningful.

Sometimes it's easy to be intuitive about a ministry's purpose just by understanding its strategy. Usually these ministries are successful financially. Child sponsorship is a prime example: "My thirty dollars will feed one child for one month."

But many worthy causes are harder to grasp. As a grant-maker, I had to be intuitive about financing an exploratory trip by a few American seminary professors to India to discuss the facilitation of a PhD program in missiology. No such thing existed at the time. The professors had to help me understand that in the scheme of things, distinct cultures need a coterie of scholars to explore what will work best for evangelization in their own context. The *strategy* of creating a PhD program within a cultural context was a method to achieve a larger *purpose*—to evangelize a culture.

How Do I Know I'm Doing It?

How will I know I'm accomplishing what God has called me do?

The answer to this question often leads to wild arm-waving statements, with outcomes extrapolated from dreams and desires rather than the conceptual ideas indicating that you're really moving toward your destination. It's the difference between saying, "By the year 2020 we'll plant twenty thousand churches," and saying, "By God's grace, where He leads, we'll be training and deploying teams of evangelists and church planters, and these churches will in turn be doing the same." (Both of those sentences come from vision statements I've read.)

Quantitative measurements can be an important part of your overall understanding of your work—but they're *not* part of your vision and purpose statement.

Facing Barriers

These three questions essentially answer the following: need, calling, and an indicator of outcomes to be achieved. Taken together, they're a holy nexus achieved by prayer and guided by the Holy Spirit toward a destination God wants you to pursue.

Together, they form the vision statement for your ministry. Givers join you at this point of vision, as do all the other people you need, such as personnel, volunteers, and endorsers. For godly planning, your strategies—those efforts you need money and resources for—will arise from the answers to these three questions.

The answers will help draw others to join you on the journey and give you the true joy of partnership, even when you experience trials.

You'll always know whether something belongs in your plans if you understand your vision. Sometimes barriers get in the way. Barriers can include circumstances in which God is redirecting you or Satan is trying to stop you. But they can also be merely an obstacle—great or small—that you simply must get past. Knowing your purpose is critical to the discernment you will need when the inevitable barriers come up that you will face in the accomplishment of your calling. A barrier could be the failure to execute your strategies effectively. Another could be your lack of understanding about some important factor related to your mission.

Having a solid grasp of your vision will help you discern the nature of these barriers; that is, knowing the answer to these questions helps you know when to surmount a wall or to turn away from a barrier God may have set in place. Opposition, hardship, struggle, mistakes, sin, incompetence, unforeseen circumstances, unintended consequences, even outright persecution—all these and more can erect barriers to moving forward in your task.

Someone wise in leadership once told me, "Take advantage of your advantages." Well, here's our great advantage: we have the Holy Spirit as our counselor. No financial advantage, no educational advantage, no experience advantage—nothing life has to offer—is more meaningful for acquiring practical, useful wisdom than asking the Holy Spirit for it. That doesn't mean an education or money or experience aren't helpful or even necessary—if you have them, they're building blocks for accomplishing what God leads you to do. But your ministry begins with the

Holy Spirit, and your starting place is prayer and expectation.

Accessing the Holy Spirit as our counselor is what distinguishes us and our work. As Jesus tells us, "Ask and it will be given to you; seek and you will find; knock and the door will be opened to you" (Matt. 7:7).

When Vision Gets Down to Work

When I worked at the Rescue Mission, God prepared me for the challenges I would later encounter as a grant-maker. It is where He taught me how to trust Him and others.

When I started speaking in churches to help raise funds for the Mission's operations, understanding the answers to the three questions above helped me articulate the purpose of our Mission, but it wasn't easy, and I made it hard on Lewis.

A few months after that, I started the job as Mission administrator. I came to understand its problems intimately—and to me they were legion. So much so, I made a list. It went to nearly two full pages, single-spaced, on a yellow pad. I invited Lewis to my apartment to break the news and see what he would do. It wasn't that I wanted to challenge him; I was just bewildered by what we faced, and I was somewhat self-righteous about my findings.

As I ticked off the points on my list, Lewis moved wordlessly to the edge of his seat, nodding his head in an oddly sad way that seemed to say with each new problem explained, "I agree."

My words fell like hammer blows, until suddenly, before I got halfway through my first page, Lewis collapsed onto the floor in a sobbing heap, crying out to the Lord, "All I ever wanted to do was win souls for You."

Stunned—and never feeling more like the young punk

I was—I sensed I was on holy ground looking at the first true saint I'd ever encountered. I fell to my knees. All I could say was, "We'll make this work." I repeated it again and again. Several things happened to me in that moment. I became the follower I was supposed to be. I also resolved that when encountering challenges, I would try to think of solutions, and I would determine how I could be part of the solution.

I also learned about my spiritual gifting. For the first time I began to understand that God had given me an understanding of the incumbent challenges of process, the gift of administration.

Most importantly, I came to understand that biblical heroes are still alive today, and though I was far short of such a claim, I was in the presence of one who was deserving of the honor.

Lewis was sailing to his destination, and it was up to me to help make our boat shipshape.

Lewis's purpose and his destination were the same: to evangelize the least, the last, and the lost, and to do it God's way.

Several years later, I was granted one of the greatest honors of my life when the Whitehead family asked me to officiate at Lewis's funeral. My text that day was drawn from Matthew 5:8: "Blessed are the pure in heart, for they will see God."

Back in my early days of working with Lewis, I couldn't have explained the concept of "integral mission"; we just lived it out. Led by Lewis, we fed the hungry, clothed the naked, sheltered the homeless, and comforted the hurting. We visited the prisoner, and we preached the gospel without ceasing. And people joined in to help.

When money goes on mission

> When a ministry's purpose is a clearly defined destination, it gives direction to where money can serve on mission.

9

CHARACTER

Being Someone Others Trust
and Its Impact on Giving and Receiving

YOU WOULDN'T NORMALLY think of a brick as a symbol of love and courage, but I have an old red one that is exceptionally ordinary, weathered, and entirely without value. It is an Ebenezer for me; literally, a brick of remembrance about the power of love and the courage needed to love like Jesus.

I picked it out of a bulldozed pile of similar bricks that had been the home of the Rescue Mission. The original Mission home had met this fate because the city leaders had decided that getting rid of the Mission would get rid of their homeless problem. The injustice and downright foolishness of their approach deeply angered me, especially when one of the city leaders, previewing what was going to happen, had stuck his finger in my face in an expression of frustration at our reluctance to go along with his plan, and hissed, "We're closing you down, and that's it!"

I walked out of his office and through the darkened corridors of City Hall late that night determined to get revenge. After all, we were serving the poorest of the poor. Both daily newspapers in our area had editorialized in favor of the Mission and we had growing support in the local Christian community and

also from opposition politicians who fought for justice and poverty programs. A variety of others supported us as well, among
whom was an organization that offered to finance a lawsuit on
our behalf.

And I was about to deploy them all, including a large bill-
board on the side wall of the Mission depicting the aforementioned leader driving a bulldozer knocking it down.

But love stopped me in my tracks.

When I told Lewis of my exchange with this man and my
plans for securing justice, he fixed a look on me that I took to
express the sentiment, "My dear child, what will it take to make
you understand?" followed by the firm instruction, "No, we're
going to love our city, not fight it or embarrass it."

"Love the city? How more wrong could he be?" I thought.
Yet, I was the one that was wrong. Love actually worked, but it
came with a price. When we chose—or better said, when Lewis
chose—*not* to press our advantages and to seemingly place our
collective head on the executioner's guillotine, I knew it was
all over.

It was an unusually rainy Monday late afternoon when the
city decided to pass the resolution to close us down. Soon after, a
local Christian radio station, KYMS, broadcast an editorial con-
demning the action. Apparently God organized the rest, because
I didn't.

Driving to City Hall for the hearing, I felt my mood darken
as I saw the rain and thought, "Can it get any worse than this?" It
was a rhetorical question, not a prayer, but I got an answer that
I didn't understand. In my spirit, I sensed the words, "It doesn't
rain on My army." When I finally got near City Hall, I understood,

as my way was blocked by a crowd numbering into the thousands and an exasperated police chief who hadn't planned on a demonstration of any size. Neither had I. Nonetheless, the crowd was actually organized by a group of women I didn't know who had tables set up and were passing out little yellow Save the Mission stickers. When I finally made my way through the crowd, I saw five of the seven city council members wearing Save the Mission stickers, and without any presentation on our part, the mayor bowed to the pressure of his surprised colleagues and set up a commission to "study" the issue.

After two solid years of weekly meetings with a variety of government officials, we finally had our solution: the Mission was to close and reopen once I could build the new one on a disputed piece of property adjacent to "Murder Central." The result was that after the two years it had taken me to figure out how to finance the project, get it built, and survive the lawsuits and protests, we finally prevailed. The literal cost of loving the city will never be fully understood; however, there is no doubt uncounted lives and souls were lost. The folks God had called us to serve were the sort that had a hampered ability to pursue opportunities for help; for the most part, opportunities had to pursue them, just like we're taught in Jesus' parable of the lost sheep. The Mission was their way up and out of the street. It was a heartbreaking time. Yet today, the legacy of Lewis's decision can be seen in the incredible range and work of the present-day Mission, which accomplishes more in a single day than we could then in our best month.

Thirty-five years later, I passed on this lesson to a young man. Mark was the newly installed president of a wonderful, but flailing, ministry in need of a new and talented leader. Leaving a secure and fruitful position with a highly respected ministry, Mark had accepted the position, a decision that could be seen as either foolhardy or anointed. On the day he started, he had no more than a couple of months of operating revenue in the bank, an exhausted fundraising effort, and a looming stack of unpaid bills.

Soon, Mark faced his toughest challenge. As the ministry's funding continued to falter, his best hope of getting the money necessary to reverse the ministry's descent seemed to hinge on a partner ministry that was fundraising for his ministry's field projects. Facing funding issues of their own, the partner ministry held back on a promised transfer of designated funds, which should have forced Mark's ministry to close down critical field operations. It didn't. His ministry courageously fulfilled its commitment to the community and finished the program as designed, relying on God to provide the needed funds from other sources. He did.

The tension caused Mark to fall into the same binary trap I experienced three decades earlier when I thought the only option to save the Mission was to pursue our opposition with vigilance. Making matters worse, the atmosphere had grown adversarial between the two ministries. Despite his fear that being unsuccessful could finally signal the end for the ministry, Mark chose the courageous path, and love won. He and the ministry board forgave the debt.

It turns out, the partner ministry hadn't actually raised the funds they had promised and were near death themselves. Both ministries limped away from the struggle with Mark's in a far more precarious position. Over the next few months, Mark and his small team began to scratch out a day-to-day living for the work, slowly gaining traction. Today, as of this writing, the ministry, with Mark at the helm, has exemplary programs and is deploying multiple millions of dollars in innovative, sustainable autochthonous community development programs complemented with a dynamic and expanding reach for the gospel.

Mark credits the moment he and his board decided to love their "adversary" and offer the grace they would have wanted and needed if the situation was reversed, to the blessed reach of their mission today. This outcome would not have occurred without a deep measure of love and the courage of Mark and his board to act on it. That love defines character and serves as an example for all of us. This is why this section of this book follows the previous chapter on purpose: without character, purpose is meaningless. Godly character in both givers and receivers is the key attribute needed for God-honoring ministry.

GODLY CHARACTER IN BOTH GIVERS AND RECEIVERS IS THE KEY ATTRIBUTE NEEDED FOR GOD-HONORING MINISTRY.

Earning Trust

When outstanding character is obvious in a mission leader and those working with him, givers know, *"This is someone we can trust. This is someone we can work with."* As a result, communion occurs because givers enter into a partnership with leaders they can trust.

Trustworthiness is certainly one of the most critical

elements of having good character; and, correspondingly, breaking trust leads to a reputation of flawed character that is very difficult to overcome.

Consider endorsements. They are a critical element when learning about someone's character. A good endorsement, from an independent source, truthfully conveyed, can go a long way to answer the question about one's character. A questionable endorsement can be a kiss of death.

Some time ago, I considered a proposal from an organization I didn't really know but that had an impressive group of people listed on its letterhead. Even though the grant request wasn't necessarily compelling, the reference list was, and I knew one of the people on the list quite well. So I called him to ask him about the organization and the grant request.

Three problems became immediately apparent. First, the person I called was unaware that the proposed project was the key program of the ministry for which he was listed as a reference; second, he was unaware that I was being contacted about the project; and third, judging by the long silence that greeted my question about the project, he didn't really believe in its potential.

This call created a situation that went badly for the grantee—a situation that could have been avoided. It didn't go so well for my acquaintance either.

I'm pretty sure the grantee didn't expect me to call anyone on the board of reference list on their letterhead, and even worse, he didn't expect that such a call would go badly for him.

If you're a mission leader and you gather a list of endorsers or establish a board of reference, make sure the people you name have a thorough understanding of what you're doing, that they like what you're doing, and that you know what they're going to say to others about you. The same qualifications apply to people you choose for a board of directors, your staff, and key volunteers.

Have you ever noticed how fast bad news travels and how slow good news spreads? I've looked at this in many ways, and my best guess is that perhaps bad news is, sadly, more interesting or useful. One thing I do understand: a good reputation is hard earned; it's also easy for gossip to destroy it. The other thing I'm sure of: all that's required from you and your organization is to be courageous, do your work, be accountable, give honest reports, and keep your word.

Getting to Know You

If at some point in your work you find yourself part of an effort to obtain a foundation grant, questions such as the following should be part of the process of getting to know you:

- Who knows your work and would serve as a reference?
- Can you be trusted?
- Are you known for your follow-through?
- Are you a learner? In your organization's pursuit of excellence, is there a mindset of studying failures and questioning successes, and then making improvements in your operations based on what you learn?
- If a gift is improperly given or offered, will you risk saying no to it, no matter its size?

Risk, Reward, and Necessary Change

In the familiar Parable of the Talents found in Matthew and
Luke, we have a direct lesson from Jesus about fear, risk-taking,
and courage. Wise servants—stewards of the Master's resources
—are given money to invest according to their ability. Two of
the servants, one with five portions or talents and, the other
with ten, were sent out in pursuit of profit. The third was given
one talent, and because of the fear of retribution if he failed, he
buried his talent so he could return it intact to the master. The
others, taking significant, if not calculated risks, doubled their
master's investment.

Risk assumes both reward and failure. What if the two who
were successful had failed? Would the master have been angry if
they were all in, used their wisdom to its fullest, and still failed?
Based on my experience with the Master, the answer would be
an emphatic *no*.

In giving and receiving, how do we become wise stewards?
Start with courage. What does this mean for you and those in
your organization? How squarely do you face reality? As a mission leader, do you confront things as they really are, not as you
hope them to be or project them as being?

To me, being wise stewards means being diligent in continually striving to understand the times and dynamics of the situation you've been called to change. This may seem obvious, but if
your givers and your board, and even your key staff, are focused
on a certain way of doing things that's apparently successful,
questioning that success can bring on a massive organizational
headache.

If your givers are still responding, and if your field reports are accurate and somewhat predictable, why change? Even a modest amount of inertia is comforting at times. However, often without really noticing it, things can begin to drift downward. A few givers drop off, then a few more, and everyone buckles down and tightens up on the spending.

An easy answer may be sought. You may think, "Oh, it's just a downturn in the economy." Maybe you put a little more thought into the diminishing fund balance, and you determine, "We'll have to be more intentional in our fundraising; perhaps we should hire a development director or put a Donate Here button on our website." Or when the home office depends on the percentage of income they receive from missionary support raising, the need for money may divert mission energy away from innovation and toward further recruiting, which may put a greater demand on existing missionaries to up their monthly support raising and, in turn, the money the home office will receive as a percentage.

Other easy answers may require a shift in field emphasis away from a traditional program to one that givers are moving toward; for example, away from orphans and toward prostitute rescue. Perhaps personnel will be shuffled.

Changes like these may all be warranted, and you may think, "After all, there's a place for incremental change for the sake of adjusting and improving." However, incremental change often becomes the enemy of real and necessary change. To understand what's actually going on, it takes a leader whose heart is prepared by prayerfully seeking the counsel of the Holy Spirit.

Recently, I observed how a large, multinational, well-respected ministry was laboring under an organizational structure that might have made sense when they were founded in the nineteenth century, but that over time had created an entrenched and entitled structure that was now a major drain on limited resources, as well as a barrier to field innovation. It took a courageous leader who was willing to risk her job to meet the challenge of significantly revamping the organization over several years, moving it into a place of effective ministry in the twenty-first century.

Ignoring the situation or hoping that it would change on its own were not options for this leader. Prayerfully, with counsel and the support she had earned from other leaders in the organization, she sensed God was moving her to question the structure she'd inherited and to embrace the challenge of bringing change.

Although bringing about the needed change was challenging, her courage and hard work paid off, and the ministry became much stronger after the process was completed.

Expect Opposition

Sometimes opposition is disguised as good ideas that are not necessarily God's ideas. One of the most prevalent good ideas that causes mission drift is a strategic funding plan based on setting up small businesses to fund core operations rather than simply exploring new fundraising opportunities. Autochthonous leaders and their supporters often fall victim to this clever diversion from their core mission. It sounds logical. "Look," a leader might explain, "there aren't many churches here, and the financial poverty is so pervasive where we work that if you help us start this simple business we can fund the work going forward."

There are many things wrong with this idea. For one, I've

never known of a business person anywhere who, when starting a business, wasn't totally consumed with seeking success and avoiding failure. Starting a business to support a ministry, even with volunteers to staff it, can drain significant energy from the actual mission of the ministry.

AUTOCHTHONOUS LEADERS AND THEIR SUPPORTERS OFTEN FALL VICTIM TO THE "START A SMALL BUSINESS" DIVERSION.

Michael, mentioned in the first chapter, was one such man. He kept his shop going as best he could while trying to overcome the lack of funds needed for his growing ministry. Once he grasped the idea that he needed instead to focus on his relationships with the local Christian community, no matter how few in number they were or how financially beleaguered, things began to turn around for his ministry.

This is an example of the Living Stones idea worked out in real time. You must never think that your church is too poor to act. Think that and you deny your church members the same discipling experience all Christians that give have experienced over two millennia of Christian expansion.

For these reasons, I've come to see this idea as a distraction formulated by the prince of lies. Wait a second, you might say, what if getting a job or starting a business is exactly how God wants the ministry to achieve its funding, rather than traditional funding? If you are to start a business, then pour your total effort into that. To do otherwise is like trying to ride two horses at the same time. If you're a circus performer, it's possible, but it's unnecessarily difficult.

Opposition also comes in the form of persecution.

There are many examples of biblical heroes who displayed courage in Scripture, even while their weaknesses were likewise on display—heroes such as Elijah and David and many others. They stood, ran, or hid in the face of persecution, or they took the battle against evil directly to the enemy. These honest portraits help us identify with the humanness and triumph of these heroes God raised up.

Why is it important to spend time looking at courage in a book about fundraising and giving? The answer is because the actions of giving and receiving are about being nimble and resourced enough to face the uncertain demands of the actual future.

When a financial giver partners with a ministry leader on the journey toward a ministry's destination, the giver must have confidence that the ministry's leadership will do the right thing in the face of opposition. If not, why would a giver entrust the ministry's leaders with the money that God gave him or her to steward?

What's presented to a giver in a proposal, or any type of request for funds, is a glimpse, really just representative of a single moment in time, of a point of view looking forward. The proposal will present your vision, which will give context to the idea you're hoping will be funded, as well as all the necessary particulars to make what you're hoping to do with the money understandable.

What you're planning to do may have a long track record of proven success, but we all know that before the ink is dry on a proposal, much less before the giver has time to react, Satan may already be conspiring against you. Scripture tells us he's a roaring lion seeking to devour us. If you're truly shining light into the darkness he has created, you'll attract opposition. And that opposition will be directed at the disruption of your plans, people, and resources.

It would be nice if Satan showed up in a red body suit with little horns, smelling of sulfur, and carrying a pitchfork, but he doesn't. Scripture tells us he's a beautiful creature and the father of clever lies. He can whisper and cajole. He'll attempt to defeat or shoot arrows of fear into your heart that can weaken your knees and cause you to face suffering so intense it clouds your judgment. That's why we have a deep need to be sustained in ministry through prayer.

But Satan's tactics are not the only things that can impact the veracity of a proposal as you move into the projected future. No, our own fallibility follows us around like our shadow. Mistakes are a common part of all our lives. Even a single mistake can accompany the boldest risk-taker like an insistent talker on a long journey. The best of us fail under the weight of our own decisions, sometimes many times, before a glimmer of success appears on the horizon.

It's a wonder we get anything done, but we do. That's the nature of things when you work in the harvest and have the Holy Spirit as your counselor.

Rewarding, But Not Easy

To the giver, the character of whoever he or she funds is therefore paramount. Givers ask, "Are they courageous? Will they be truthful? Do they follow through? Can they manage their team without destroying them? Do they learn from their mistakes? Will they ask the tough questions? Do they submit themselves to an accountability structure? Do they lead in such a way that their ministry is bathed in prayer?"

Good answers to these questions allow givers to trust, so that ministry leaders can not only meet the challenges they planned for, but the ones that actually unfold.

Maybe you're a ministry leader already beset by too many necessary things to do with too little time to do them. If so and you're wondering, "How can I take the time to get these answers?" or "How can I actually let a giver get that close to me?" Sing hallelujah! for your salvation draws near. Faith-based courage shines when there are no easy answers.

When money goes on mission

> . . . character is what burns the dross out of the transactional nature of giving and receiving. It longs for community and disciplines the use of money to its best and most useful Kingdom service.

10

IDEAS

Unlocking Funding for Your Strategies

PURPOSE LEADS to strategies, and strategies are nothing more than our best ideas of how to reach a mission's destination; that is, how to accomplish its calling.

In the world of missions, a lot of emphasis is placed on long-term planning. It sounds about right. After all, how are you going to get anywhere if you don't know how you're going to get there?

Don't overcomplicate things by spending too much time on long-term planning. I've been as guilty of this as anyone, and it didn't make me a better leader or cause me to lead efforts with better results.

I'm not saying don't plan. You do need to plan. In fact, your near-term planning is absolutely critical to reaching your long-term goals and your destination. But long-term planning can also and waste time.

My friend Roger Parrott has caused a few mind-bending moments for me over the years, including when I briefly worked for him as US Lausanne director just after the second Lausanne Congress in Manila.

I first met Roger when he was fundraising for that Congress, which was held in 1989. At the time, I was working for an unincorporated private foundation, and I'd become accustomed to high-powered pitches for mission funding. But nothing prepared me for meeting Roger.

He came into my office like a force of nature. He was young, ruddy of face, friendly, and very focused. Roger had taken on the incredible task of raising seven million dollars to put on the Congress, which, at the time, was just eighteen months away. Usually, there is hardly anything interesting about funding a large international meeting. Believe me, it is a steep hill to climb for most fundraisers, but it wasn't for Roger. Somehow, he motivated us to give him the grant he was seeking.

But this wasn't the mind-bending moment that brings me to the point of this story. No, that came twenty-one years later, in Cape Town, South Africa, during the third Lausanne Congress when Roger presented a workshop titled "Long-Term Planning for Your Ministry Is a Waste of Time."

It happened during a brief forty-five-minute session he presented in a dark corner of a cavernous ballroom designed for a group fifty times bigger than the thirty of us huddled together. We heard Roger destroy the shibboleth of long-term planning and its perception as being so true and so wise that it wasn't to be questioned. Roger questioned it.

Roger is the president of Belhaven University. University presidents live and die with long-term plans for how to expand their campuses, develop new programs, build student bodies, and impress accrediting agencies. Additionally, accrediting agencies and trustee boards demand long-term planning to project growth toward even more excellence. In my own coaching at the time, I taught that long-term planning was one key to motivating givers.

Those of us listening to Roger that day were dubious at best about the claim asserted in the title of his workshop. But he cogently explained how long-term plans are hardly ever useful once they are completed, they drain a lot of staff energy to come up with them, and they tend to homogenize a team's gifts. One more point especially got my attention: Roger said that long-term planning can displace a ministry's ability to take advantage of opportunities in response to future events and change.

Of course! The ministries I coached and helped to get grants were always encountering changing dynamics in their work.

Suddenly, I whipped out my notebook and pen and began to take furious notes as Roger kept talking. It was a moment of blinding insight for me.

ROOTED IN REALITY

I had admired Roger's walk with Christ and his excellence and success as a college president. Now he was giving me unexpected insight into his pattern of work. This was not a man driven to bend events to his will—a driver who calculated his every move and swept away every obstacle in his path. Instead, I was encountering something much more nuanced and really much godlier in approach.

I knew donors were attracted to vision, but I'd been teaching and coaching that long-term planning helped give context to how their gifts would be useful, thus giving the donor a sense of purpose, even though I'd often seen how egregious uses of this idea could lead to crazy declarations in proposals, even by godly, well-meaning leaders. These proposals had five-year or ten-year

plans with wonderfully drawn round-numbered goals encapsu-
lated in terms like this: "Our 20/20 vision in five years will have
200 regional training hubs, deploying 2,000 evangelists to plant
20,000 churches by the year 2020." In all the proposals I've read,
I can't remember encountering something that read more like
this: "In three years, seven months, and twenty-six days, we plan
to reach 172 villages with the word of Christ—leaving behind
thirty-seven church planters establishing perhaps a new church
every eighteen months." Long-term plans seem to demand easy-
to-understand outcomes—clear statements, like flags you send
up a tall pole for everyone to salute.

I should note that Roger believes in very tight planning
within the visible horizon, where there's a reasonable chance of
accomplishing goals. He believes strongly in being led by God
and in planning to take advantage of unforeseen opportunities
that reward excellence and effort. In my own practice, I now
teach the importance of planning tightly for the next eighteen
months to two years and the need for regular feedback set within
a clear understanding of the destination God has set out for you.

Embedded in a drive to delineate succinct long-term goals
is a desire to get at clear, measurable outcomes. It has something
to do with accountability. Was Roger saying we should throw all
that out the window?

The questions that day came fast and furious. Meanwhile, I
was mapping out a whole new approach to understanding what
motivates givers—an approach that in the succeeding years has
immeasurably improved my work. I didn't throw out all the old,
but simply brought my thinking into compliance with the real
world God has us working in—a world where we can seek a

communion of giving and receiving between the giver and the mission leader. It's a world where truth and real partnership are the norm, and where failure and success can be equally embraced, studied, and questioned. It's a world where givers and mission leaders share outcomes because they're on the journey together.

Roger had bent my mind to envision something I'd only dreamed was possible. I'd seen it work in fits and starts. Now I was going to encourage God-shaped ambitions, not ambitions that were shaped because they were *thought* to be God-sized.

I now had a new challenge: *How do I explain all this?* The answer came after a time of reflection, when I asked an obvious question of myself, "Just what did I really think about when evaluating a new potential grantee for my employer?"

The answer could take you on what might be an unfamiliar journey for you, a journey into the mind of a former program officer for an evangelical charitable foundation focused on missions giving.

Good Examples of Strategic Planning

For me, it all starts by understanding the powerful distinction between good ideas and "God ideas." All God-inspired ideas are good ones; however, some good ideas—ideas that succeed in achieving goals—can be powerfully destructive or have unintended negative consequences that don't honor God. That's why I place the emphasis on knowing that your purpose is from God before lining out your plans to achieve it.

After reading countless proposals, I can truly say that most contain aspirational goals masked as strategic plans. And with

THERE IS A POWERFUL DISTINCTION BETWEEN GOOD IDEAS AND "GOD IDEAS."

good cause, because true strategic planning is tough.

The best strategic planners I know of are third-grade teachers. Seriously. They have to take a gaggle of eight year olds and shape them into nine year olds, who must be prepared for critical thinking and the ability to communicate complex thoughts. They must be ready for a fourth-grade year that will inundate their young brains with an information dump of epic proportions, including history, arithmetic, spelling, and manners—at least that's how I remember it.

My wife, who at one time was a teacher, is an outstanding strategic planner. I used to marvel at how tightly she planned a school year. She knew exactly where her students needed to be at the end of the year, and by testing at the beginning of the year she found out how far they were from that goal. Each day was carefully planned to move them along. Yet, out of necessity, she remained completely flexible in executing her plans—simply because students learn at different rates. She constantly tested and adjusted as she went, and, judging by her popularity with her colleagues who would teach her students in the future, she did an excellent job of getting the students ready for their yearly transitions. In something I relate to, she worked doubly hard with the late bloomers to help every one of them to move on. Now that's genuine strategic planning that produces results.

I once had a board member who led a team in developing deep-water submersible vehicles. This man did the most intricate planning I've ever encountered. At his business, there was a large conference room lined from head level to knee level with a PERT chart that rolled out all the steps necessary—hourly and daily for more than three years—in order to get a submersible vehicle to go from design to launch. Deviations such as accidents, late deliverables, bad weather—you name it—were highlighted in red as they occurred and changed the launch date, which was written in chalk on a blackboard in the corner, as if to remind everyone of the impact of the deviations.

Now that's planning on a level that most mere mortals like me can't fathom.

Both these examples of strategic planning are actual true measurements of results, and each wasted no time on a step that didn't move along to the desired goal.

It's good to remember that givers love your purpose—that's why they join with you in funding your plans. However, the emphasis in most proposals is on how the money needed will be spent. The problem is that most plans, when seen as a stand-alone item, are less than compelling if they don't present the context of how your ideas and their necessary tactics fulfill your purpose.

For the schoolteacher, the purpose relates to children who'll need to be well-rounded grown-ups someday needing jobs. For the team developing deep-water submersible vehicles, the purpose was producing a seaworthy boat that somebody is willing to pay a lot of money for to look at things on the sea floor. For our work at the Rescue Mission, the purpose was having a useful facility that gave us a chance to express Christ's love for the least, the last, and the lost.

Yet, most of the tactics or strategies needing funding to fulfill these purposes were prosaic at best—a janitor to mop the showers at the Mission, a welder to build the submarine, and books for the teacher to use. How do you make these things interesting?

Placing them in the context of your purpose is the answer. By making sure you communicate how these strategies will serve your purpose, you provide wonderful background music to your investors and to all who'll join you on your journey.

No matter how small your staff or your team of volunteers, each of your strategies should have a person assigned to oversee it and manage its feedback loop.

To understand a feedback loop, picture a circle with four equally spaced points. The four points are marked "Plan," "Do," "Measure," and "Change." At regular intervals, every strategy should move through this circular process. By doing this, you give yourself and your ministry the best chance of keeping your ideas current and effective.

Bathed in prayer, this is the means for disciplining yourself and your team to study failure and to question success.

The whole idea of questioning success can be perplexing. Why do that? As the saying goes, "if it ain't broke, don't fix it." You're thinking, stay the course; there'll be plenty of time in the future to make necessary changes.

But the problem is that some changes happen *to* you; they're not made *by* you. Let's say you're a church planter and your efforts have produced results faster than you anticipated. If your strategy didn't account for this, it's possible that you might find yourself having to leave the churches in the hands of untrained leadership. That's a change in your strategy—but not one you either wanted or planned for.

Understanding Change

I once sat in a meeting with a group of autochthonous pastors who'd just gained the freedom in their country to lead services openly. They were meeting with a Westerner who'd just been installed as the new leader of a multifaceted agency that had worked in the country for more than twenty-five years. They had established a major hospital as well as other outreaches.

This was a difficult meeting for the Westerner, whose agency hadn't produced a doctor from the local culture or even developed any of the local Christians as leaders. The agency hadn't planned for the day when their autochthonous brothers and sisters could openly take responsibility and ownership of their own work or even be able to take key leadership positions directing the work and overseeing employees of the various Western missions they represented.

The problem might have been that his agency had only focused on the strategy of healing but lacked a strategy for creating sustainability both in funding for the hospital and staffing. The problem could have boiled down to the fact that it took less effort to recruit Western doctors than to develop local ones. These were fine, sacrificial people who were trying to do their best for the least, the last, and the lost they were called to. But they failed to see perhaps the most strategic need in front of them: to give leadership to autochthonous Christians.

Another time, I attended a conference that sought to look into the future decade and to have a round-table discussion about how to adapt each agency's plans to the coming changes in a major country. The featured speaker was a US State Department expert on that particular country and was also an evangelical Christian. He laid out two plausible but diametri-cally-opposed potentialities for missions wanting to be effective over the span of the next ten years. In one, the country's military would close it up more tightly than it already was; in the other, the doors would be flung open to the West to do business—and, by inference, mission.

I was at the meeting as an observer. Looking back now, the presenter was prescient. The country opened up, yet at the meet-ing in the succeeding days after the presentation, the agencies didn't ac-count for either of the eventualities in their planning or presentations. Without exception, they focused on doing more of the same in some muddled, fuzzy middle ground that didn't signal any understanding that change of some sort was inevitable.

> YOUR STRATEGIES ARE YOUR IDEAS DRAWN LOGICALLY FROM YOUR PURPOSE.

Your strategies are your ideas drawn logically from your pur-pose. In and of themselves, strategies may not be that interesting, but seen in the context of your purpose, they can become glow-ing embers of passion in their creative application to fulfill your God-given calling—your purpose.

If you're led of God, givers will fund your strategies as they grasp their impact on your purpose.

When money goes on mission

... it funds the strategies of a ministry's purpose. The purpose gives context to the ideas about how to do ministry. Givers fund strategies, but they are drawn to the work of the ministry because they seek the same destination or purpose. Giving money is their way to serve this purpose.

11

TRACK RECORD

Looking Back to Look Forward

YOUR TRACK RECORD is simply a way of looking back to look forward. If you're a mission leader making a proposal to obtain a grant, your track record represents the substance of your promise, not your promise itself.

If your idea is intriguing to a giver, then your demonstrated track record will be helpful in determining the appropriate size of the gift and whether you can be expected to be successful.

As a grant-maker, once I learned that a mission's strategy was compelling in light of their vision and where they were working—and once I'd determined they had good character that I could trust—I next evaluated their track record. I especially wanted to know what they'd already accomplished, not what they were hoping to do. This also helped me to determine how to shape my funding recommendation. A limited track record, say of a new work, might only warrant a small grant at the start, whereas a longer track record could

A MINISTRY'S TRACK RECORD PLAYS A SIGNIFICANT ROLE IN GRANT-MAKING.

be considered for a larger one. A ministry's track record plays a significant role in grant-making.

LIVING IT OUT

Twenty years ago, a number of my colleagues, leaders and program officers at US granting foundations, were struggling to understand how to participate in the great growth of new believers and churches in the north of India. Specifically, in our discussions, we realized we had similar challenges in knowing which seminaries and colleges in India were geared up to meet the incredible demand for the new leaders this movement of God had created.

We decided to organize a campaign to learn what we needed to know. David Bennett, who serves on the board of First Fruit and earned his PhD at Fuller Seminary studying Indian leadership patterns, led the program we called The India Leadership Study. Ten foundations and one mission organization participated and shared the costs of the study.

David began the research by going to trusted and respected Indian leaders, asking them whom he should seek out. Beginning with those few recommended, he asked each of them to recommend several additional ministries he should look at. When he received multiple recommendations of the same institution or ministry, he conducted an on-site visit to learn about the organization. Eventually, he compiled a list of 112 vetted ministries, working in five varieties of leadership development, from the preparation of lay leadership to programs focused on developing national and regional leaders. At the end of the study, the results were shared at a conference organized by leaders throughout India who wanted to know what David had learned. Those of us involved in the study learned that David was a beloved outsider, the kind of researcher who is trusted, impartial, and comes with a different viewpoint.

In the five years following the study, it was estimated that more than $55 million in grants were given. Today, The Indian Collaboration, a picture of communion between receivers and givers, is a fellowship jointly led by a wider circle of foundations and major donors, both Westerners and Indians, which is financed by both groups and is a continuation of the original study.

This nice story has a point. The entirety of the original study was built by David discovering and authenticating the track records of the original 112 ministries. Some had stellar records; some didn't. Some were longstanding, well regarded stalwarts of the Indian church. Others were hardly known outside of their neighborhoods. For the most part, each ministry received grants according to its known ability and *potential*.

SOMETIMES TRACK RECORD ONLY POINTS TO POTENTIAL. THAT'S WHY IT'S IMPORTANT TO LIVE OUT GOOD CHARACTER, YOUR PURPOSE, AND YOUR IDEAS.

Yes, sometimes track record only points to potential. That's why it's so important to possess and live out, as best you can, good character, your purpose, and your ideas.

Even a bad track record can help you get a grant. In 1983, just after I started working in philanthropy, I recommended my first grant. It might well have been, despite my inexperience, one of the best I have ever worked on.

It happened when I met Phill Butler, a serial entrepreneur, a driver, a mentor . . . and now a longtime friend. He founded InterCristo (a mission job-seeking service); InterDev (focused on developing partnerships between missions working in the same field); and VisionSynergy (a ministry applying partnership training and facilitation to missions, networks, and movements). Phill started InterDev when he was in his sixties.

Phill began the meeting by telling me he had exhausted funds from a previous startup grant. He was given the grant to organize missions broadcasters focused on reaching listeners in a communist country. Phill had attempted to help the broadcasters coordinate schedules, programming, and azimuth (the direction and aim of short-wave broadcasts) in order to eliminate overlap and focus their evangelistic efforts.

Although this first effort had failed, Phill was undaunted. He was convinced his idea was the right one; he just hadn't executed it as well as he could have. He explained this to me in excruciating detail. He'd prepared a fourteen-page, single-spaced report on what had gone wrong, what he'd learned, and how he had now developed a better plan.

The sheer doggedness of the effort might have been enough to cause us to go forward with the second grant. A more risk-adverse philanthropy may not have done so, but we did. He got the money, despite the track record of this failure, because he had so thoroughly diagnosed what had gone wrong that it actually made us confident he would get it right the next time.

This time Phill's plan worked—spectacularly.

When you go from being flat on the canvas, having blown through a large wad of money, and you get up delivering a knockout punch—that's dramatic. It's the sort of drama that even people with a passing interest in biblical Christianity can understand.

Phill succeeded in the effort and laid the groundwork for the partnership ministries that were to follow. Through his efforts and through the countless people involved, these ministries have contributed to an explosive growth in a mission field that seemed fallow but was actually ready for great growth and harvest.

Track record is hard to fake. You can adopt someone else's purpose and shape it to your own. You can take someone else's ideas and strategies and adapt them to what you're trying to do. You can even overcome character faults with repentance and grace. But a true track record exists as a unique fact for each person and organization. It's the actual story that reveals the ministry's journey.

When you, as a mission leader, concentrate on telling everybody what you're planning on doing,

WHEN YOU CONCENTRATE ON TELLING EVERYBODY WHAT YOU'RE PLANNING ON DOING, YOU MAY SOMETIMES SKIP OVER THE MOST IMPORTANT THING THAT WILL MOTIVATE PEOPLE TO COME ALONGSIDE YOU: *WHAT HAS HAPPENED ALREADY?*

you may sometimes skip over the most important thing that will motivate people to come alongside you: *What has happened already?* Tell them the challenges you faced in your history that brought you to where you are today. This will help them understand why they should get involved with you. A mission's proven track record will build up givers' confidence.

Embedded in your story should be your "Ebenezers"—memories of when God and the Holy Spirit interacted with you in the past. They are like the remembrance stone that the prophet Samuel set up (1 Sam. 7:12) after God dramatically demonstrated His help for His people.

Ebenezers remind us that God got us through something when it didn't seem possible . . . through times of triumph when victory seems unattainable and times of sorrow when comfort comes as an unexpected grace. We all fail, and we all succeed. As a grant-maker, I was as interested in a leader's Ebenezers as in his proposal.

Share your Ebenezers. They're part of your track record. However, be careful not to take credit for the Holy Spirit's work; instead, just convey how you perceive He has worked through you and your organization.

Keep It Honest

Everyone knows the importance of a good track record. Seekers of higher-paying jobs put out a considerable effort to polish their résumés and highlight their achievements. It's natural to want to be seen in the best light. Some will even shade the truth or dispense with it altogether in an effort to gain favor. This is a constant temptation when your payroll is at stake.

As a grant-maker, I always wanted to see a fearless telling of the truth by mission leaders. I wanted to know what was really going on. I wanted to know not only if the ministry was a good fit for us but if it was a "learning" organization. Did its leaders study failure and make corrections? And, just as importantly, did they question success and make needed adjustments?

It takes a lot of trust to share that kind of information. It's easier to think, "What if our failures are embarrassing or showed an alarming lack of competence? What if we are an organization that hasn't demonstrated an ability to adjust to field realities and exploit new opportunities presented to us?"

Just about all the ministries I have encountered can tell a story of seasons where nothing seemed to be working. In life, we all fail. We all miss opportunities, even if we are never up against the pressures of a pioneering mission outreach.

I'm thankful I served in the real world of missions—that is, where failure followed me like a shadow, trouble pursued me like an enemy, and grace got me out of more fixes than I can remember. In looking for what's really going on, we know that skills, preparation, and hard work can lead to increasing success; under the grace of God, the same things can result in abject failure, for we're perfected in suffering. The most perfect gymnast still falls off the balance beam quite a lot.

When we can achieve this place of honesty in a partnership of mission and giver, we're truly in a communion of giving and receiving. I know it might seem that some grant-makers can't be trusted with the truth—perhaps because their eyes are awash with glossy storytelling from missions that seem blessed only with success and great promise of future achievements—but truth-telling is up to you. What another person does with that truth is up to them.

This is precisely where courageous leadership is called to the front. The grant-seeker provides the vision and the destination, the grant-maker resources. The better you lead, the better they follow. Earning their trust isn't easy, but it's essential.

A good track record shows how you surmounted problems, took risks, exploited opportunities, studied failures, questioned success, and harnessed the wind of God as you went about the calling on you and your organization.

But what if you don't have any track record? What if you're just getting started and you have an idea that hasn't been tried?

We've all been there. You may only have money for a salad and can only hope for a piece of chicken, but you have a Father who knows this. The salad days are just a prelude to when you get the chicken. It's in those days you'll find out if you have the courage, energy, and perseverance to achieve your calling. If you haven't been through this testing of faith, believe me, you'll remember the salad days as fondly as the ones when you finally got some meat. You don't need a rich uncle to jump start your track record, just a Father who cares and some friends to point you in the right direction.

Some years ago, I recommended a modest gift to fund a boat ferry and freight business started by African villagers. Their region was slammed with a flood so devastating it had wiped out their roads and commercial piers on a nearby lake.

The pastors of the damaged region organized a committee to ask a missionary who was working with them for help. They presented him with a business and ministry plan that outlined a request to purchase a number of outboard motors for their canoes. They asserted they could start a ferry and freight business serving their isolated communities and could also greatly expand their preaching and church planting work. Their only track record was that they were already doing it on a very limited basis, paddling everywhere they needed to go. The missionary didn't have the money to help them, but he knew an organization that could help the pastors get started by creating a non-profit holding company that could receive donations.

Nobody associated with the project had ever done anything close to what they were proposing. Yet, somehow, they came to the attention of the foundation where I was working. And we funded the start up. Admittedly, it was a compelling story. Even though this small band of autochthonous, entrepreneurial missional leaders had never run a business like this before and their proposal violated my own thoughts about missions and business, we still funded them. Why?

I remember, distinctly, being impressed that they were already doing the basic tasks of the work they were proposing to undertake. It wasn't hard to picture how the addition of outboard motors could propel the work forward. Yes, they were pastors, a class of folks not always associated with business acumen, but they were intentional to spread the gospel, and they had an impressive track record of walking or floating from place to place to preach. We admired their character, and the person who told us about them had a good reputation.

True, it's hardly ever this easy and not all of us have such a good story to share about our work, but all of us who do missional work are grafted into the vine by the Master Gardener, who also happens to be the King of kings. That's not bad to remember when starting out. He'll make a way, period.

When money goes on mission

. . . it underscores effective ministry. Effective ministry is recognized and understood by looking back at the ministry's track record and by remembering the Ebenezers of the ministry leaders.

Part 4

GIVING AND RECEIVING: FINDING TRANSFORMATION IN TRANSACTION

THE ORBIT

The Accountability
Effect on Giving and Receiving

LET'S DEMYSTIFY THE process of contemporary mission funding. When it works well, it resembles an orbit with a center that has gravitational pull and concentric rings that draw in unaligned givers from the outer edges of the mission's unique funding universe. This orbit concept, illustrated below, also provides a simple template for better understanding a proper accountability structure. Accountability encourages trust, and both are needed to create a communion of giving and receiving.

Figure 2

THE ORBIT

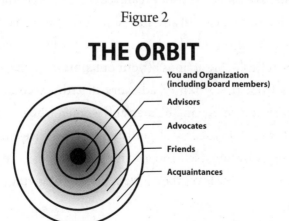

For simplicity's sake, I've divided the orbit in Figure 2 into four concentric rings with a gravitational nucleus at the center. The rings represent layers of involvement of your potential investors (acquaintances, friends, advocates, advisors). Together they make up your funding universe.

In this model, the acquaintance level, the outer ring, is where potential donors become actual givers.

The friend level is where givers begin to draw closer, making multiple gifts and perhaps gifts of a greater size while paying attention to your communication and praying for your work. The friend level is the backbone of most financially successful mission efforts.

The advocate level is where your friends take some sort of action to bring others into the orbit.

Very few givers will inhabit the next level, as advisors, because there's a changed dynamic with these donors. At this level, givers begin to develop a true second love. Not only do they love your purpose and your ultimate loving actions of the gospel, they also have a love for your organization. This is an important distinction of your closest advisors, supporters, and board members. All other givers need only to love your purpose as they seek to support the loving actions of your outcomes.

It is from the group of advisors that the accountability structure is drawn. Again, the men and women who inhabit this part of the orbit in successful, godly enterprises have two loves: for the organization itself and also for your purpose. As a demonstration of their love, they have a history of giving to your ministry.

Consider the orbit to be a picture of your funding "universe." Whether it's Christians around the world or in your immediate neighborhood, the first task is to discover that orbit. Givers need to pay attention to the ministry's funding universe as well or risk upsetting the organizational balance that is the product of sustained interdependence.

When I was fundraising for the Rescue Mission, our funding universe was California's Orange County, where nearly two million residents lived at the time. The homeless of Orange County lived on sidewalks and alleys, in cars (if they were more prosperous), or on the couches of friends (if they were still more fortunate). On a daily basis, the Mission served the five hundred homeless that were the most desperate. When we finally got our funding close to the point of parity with the work we were attempting, we were raising about one million dollars annually from a small but dedicated group of givers numbering less than two thousand investors, all from the local region.

We remained local to our setting both as responders to local needs and as fundraisers who partnered with those nearby who most clearly understood the need and were willing to participate in its solution. Interestingly, most of our givers at that time were low-income wage earners who stuck with us even through the worst of a recession that slammed the United States in the early 1980s. From that base, the work grew in size, reach, and diversity of donors.

When I fundraised for the US Lausanne Committee, the funding universe was the entire United States. In the late 1980s and early 1990s, Presbyterian churches across the nation that had a connection to Roger Parrott and others were the backbone of the fundraising effort. Later, a whole new generation of independent evangelical givers from across the world helped underwrite the historic Lausanne Movement's Congress in Cape Town in 2010. Though always an international movement, today's Lausanne leaders no longer only look to the West for underwriting the movement—their funding universe has expanded globally, as has its reach and influence.

TWO DIFFERENT FUNDING APPROACHES

The following chart shows a common approach to mission funding. When a mission field has yet to be developed, and there are no local believers in the field, then the evangelist who brings the gospel to that barren land will of necessity be bringing his support with him, either by gifts from outside supporters or by self-support or self-employment.

Figure 3

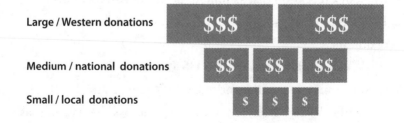

A COMMON APPROACH TO FUNDING

Large / Western donations	$$$	$$$
Medium / national donations	$$ $$ $$	
Small / local donations	$ $ $	

In the funding world, this represents an upside-down pyramid, although there's a paradigm at work that seems to make sense. It starts with a pioneering investment drawn from people with sufficient funds who aren't from the local community.

In time, however, the funding mix should switch so that local giving primarily supports the ministry. All too often, a failure to move toward local funding occurs, creating a dependency that's very hard to overcome. If there's to be a proper alignment of ownership and responsibility for local work, it's incumbent that the bulk of givers should also be local, as we see in Figure 4. When this occurs, autochthonous leaders can engage with those from outside their immediate sphere of influence as equals at the cross.

Figure 4

A NEW MODEL:
THE FUNDING PYRAMID

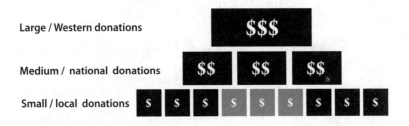

Not all missions should have regional, national, or international support. If a work of the gospel is intended to bring joy and wellness to a neighborhood, perhaps it's that neighborhood itself that should carry the bulk of the funding. On the other hand, if the work is taking on multiple neighborhoods, villages, cities, regions, even entire nations, then it follows that the universe of funding will expand correspondingly, as will the intensity of the investing and fund development work.

The Importance of Accountability

We serve God in a world that requires us to act pragmatically while we also live eternally. That's why leaders must consider whose authority they're under and seek accountability. If the receiver of funds is not in an accountability structure, the ministry will be operating with unnecessary risk. A healthy accountability structure provides the best opportunity to know God's will, keep the ministry on course, and ensure financial and programmatic health. When leaders and organizations are in healthy accountability structures, they are attractive to potential givers. This creates a trusting environment and relationship between all partners who work for and support a ministry.

Simply put, you aren't operating in an accountability structure if you answer no to the question: *Can you be fired from your position?*

In Genesis 2:15, Adam was given work to do: "The LORD God took the man and put him in the Garden of Eden to work it and take care of it." But he sinned, was cast out, and ushered mankind into an epoch of toil, pain, suffering, and death (Genesis 3). Adam was fired from his position in the garden of Eden. He was in the most perfect accountability structure that a human being has ever known. Yet the father of lies was able to trick Adam and Eve into forsaking it all (Gen. 3:1–8).

This is the second saddest story recorded in Scripture, outdone only by the crucifixion, when Jesus made the greatest sacrifice to undo the serpent's work and Adam's folly. I've seen with my own eyes how God's good work gets undone by subtle lies like Satan's; I've seen it far too often not to hammer home this point of the need for accountability in the giving and receiving of money.

However, although Adam was held accountable, he wasn't abandoned by God. Even though he and Eve felt shame at their nakedness for the first time, God provided them with clothes. Even more miraculous, we, Adam's descendants, have been restored through Christ's death (1 Cor. 15:22) and resurrection.

What does all this have to do with the communion of giving and receiving?

Everything. Even though we have God's love and forgiveness, hard work remains until all who will be saved are saved. Meanwhile, accountability is still in God's plan to keep us focused on goodness and to keep our feet securely placed on the path of righteousness.

The task of fundraising requires hard work, but it can be compared to planting a garden. If done well, in time there will be fruit—money will be raised. There's nothing quite like having others validate the calling of your mission as they give away the produce of their lives to see your God-given purpose undertaken. This brings overwhelming thankfulness all around, especially thankfulness to God.

Done in a godly manner—as Paul showed us in 2 Corinthians 8:20–21—giving brings about an emerging communion that's a significant aspect of the common bond Jesus prayed for, recorded in John 17:21. As we saw earlier, Paul raised money from the Greeks for the poor Jewish believers in Jerusalem; in doing so, he noted how such giving would provide for those in need, who in turn would provide later for the original givers in their own time of need (2 Cor. 8:14–15).

The work of fundraising is embedded in the effort to penetrate the noise of everyday life as you seek to connect with those whom God has called to your purpose. And God promises that even this work is an act of grace—particularly when it's in a balanced accountability structure.

Accountability at the Center

At the center of the orbit is the accountability structure. When this structure is in balance and working properly, it creates a gravitational pull that will draw investors or givers into the ministry's orbit.

Figure 5

ACCOUNTABILITY STRUCTURE
(Center of the Orbit)

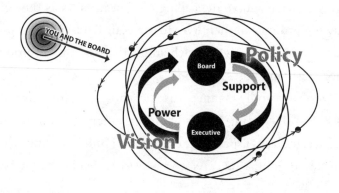

The accountability structure has four key elements and is perhaps the most important thing I've learned regarding the way godly fundraising works.

In Figure 5, the four arrows represent the dynamics that must be in balance between a mission leader (the executive) and his or her accountability structure (the board).

The "Power" arrow indicates the direction of released power that the executive gives to the board, whether the executive is the organization's founder who recruited the board members or a newly hired employee in an established ministry. The leader is under the ultimate authority of the board, even though I have encountered more than a few ministries where board members, with the authority to do so, will not or cannot, for unexpressed reasons, hold their executive accountable.

This released power of the leader (or imposed power of the board) also comes with an equally important expressed responsibility on the board's part, represented by the "Support" arrow, which points back to the leader. This responsibility is to be the covering for the executive, and ultimately for the entire mission. *Covering* is one of those strange words that can be taken to mean anything from benevolent paternalism to cosigning a loan. Rather than displaying unleashed judgment and stress-inducing criticism or indifference, the board is involved as a critical stakeholder when problems arise.

Wobbles in the orbit that throw things out of balance throughout the organization begin here when this construct of accountability and support is violated. When I've seen the wobble at its worst, it usually starts on the board side. This can come from board members being heavy-handed or clueless (which is partly the fault of the executive and the absence of development funding reviews as well as performance reviews), or from board members thinking they're only wise counselors rather than full participants and funders who are ultimately responsible for the organization's health. Conversely, I've seen boards take power and attempt to fill the executive function themselves, turning the executive into a mere functionary.

The two outermost arrows in the illustration represent two other equally important dynamics. The leader's responsibility is to give *vision* to the ministry. The corresponding responsibility of the board is to test the leader's vision and give it back to him or her as *policy*, which then becomes the executive's responsibility to carry out.

Leaders project vision and are in touch with it every day. They define the organization's reality.

The executive (as the term is used here) is often known by various other names in missions and foundations: president, executive director, general secretary, chief executive officer, team leader, and manager, among others. Boards are even more varied in name. They can be called trustees, directors, or any number of monikers in cultures where accountability as a word doesn't translate. I once worked with a group in West Africa that concluded that the concept could be best described as a tribal council—where the chief, though an unquestioned leader, serves at the pleasure of the elders.

The most dangerous threat to proper balance, health, and secure funding for an organization is when the orbit collapses— as in the more traditional client-patron model we looked at earlier. When the accountability structure is out of balance—even slightly—the effect is disruptive ripples throughout the entire donor orbit and into the mission outcomes.

A MISSION'S OVERALL HEALTH

After coaching hundreds of leaders and leading dozens of board retreats, I'm convinced that when the core accountability structure is out of balance, everything will be. Let's look at this from the perspective of the *giver* rather than the ministry leader or receiver. Picture a program officer who works for a foundation that considers money-seeking proposals from dozens or hundreds of ministries every year. Besides being secure in what God has called that officer to fund, he or she must also look at the ability of each requesting ministry to accomplish its purpose and fulfill its promises as outlined in the presented proposal.

WHEN THE CORE ACCOUNTABILITY STRUCTURE IS OUT OF BALANCE, EVERYTHING WILL BE.

Once he has determined that there's an alignment of purposes and that the organization has a satisfactory track record, is of good character, and has an idea worth funding, there's another thing to consider: the overall health of the mission organization.

When all the elements of responsible motivation for givers are in place and a communion of equals is underway, he may sense that something still seems amiss. If so, follow-up and further digging may be called for, because trusting a first impression when working across cultures is always dangerous.

Perhaps the ministry seems overly dependent on

foundations or over-dependent on North American funding. Maybe there's a slight disconnect between the mission's purpose as expressed on its website or brochures and what the program officer perceives to be its real purpose. Perhaps the ministry seems weaker financially than it should be or the executive seems to be under an inordinate amount of pressure.

Of course, as in everything, these perceptions must be measured against the truth that a perfectly run ministry and grant-making foundation doesn't exist. But it's still imperative to be alert to reality.

In my experience, when I seek to discover what's going on in situations like these, the root cause is usually some level of disconnect between the work of the board and the work of the executive. And a wobble at the center can cause serious tremors at the edges.

A Variety of Potential Challenges

When I learn of challenges in a mission organization—such as funding shortfalls, mission creep, a dispirited staff, hidebound policies that seem to be holding back new initiatives, a poverty mentality, money-centric planning, or the attempt to run a ministry organization as a family business—I look at the relationship between the executive and board and try to understand the dynamics of the wobble. To further explain, the terms I've just used in this paragraph are worth elaborating:

Funding Shortfall

I've never known a mission worth its salt that had enough money to meet all the needs before it. This seems to be the nature of poverty and injustice—and of opportunity. On the other hand, "funding shortfall" refers to a *chronic* lack of funding for initiatives and programs that are underway, often because of a breakdown in understanding the dynamic of faith and the pursuit of excellence. Or the shortfall might be because of a lack of tight short-term planning, or because long-term planning was overemphasized. Other potential causes include a wobble in the board-executive dynamic, endemic personnel issues, or lack of clarity about the need they're addressing.

Mission Creep

Mission creep occurs when the ministry's God-given calling has been compromised by taking on responsibilities that God hasn't called it to—such as the temptation to look at another calling and think, "That's where the money is," or undertaking opportunities that seemed right at the time, but only diluted the impact of the mission's true calling.

Dispirited Staff

This is often caused by a leadership style that fails to properly value a mission's employees. The leader may fail to complete development reviews or may expect too much work and sacrifice because the poor are being helped. Staff members may feel they're unable to look after their family or that they're merely in place to take orders, without being included in the decision process or valued for their contribution. Instead, staff need to be considered ambassadors for the ministry and participants in the funding process.

Poverty Mentality

Here, the leader's mindset is that the ministry is destined to be broke, or that it's "godly" to be broke. It can be the belief that it's impossible to obtain enough money for a calling to be effective. This mindset isn't to be confused with living in an incarnational way, like St. Francis, among those to whom you're called.

Hidebound Strategies and Policies

Sticking to programs simply because they exist and have a constituency is damaging because such a strategy or policy prohibits the understanding of when an idea has run its course and is no longer effective. This can stem from not discerning God's voice and from not being accountable. This situation begs for fresh thinking and a fearless approach to understanding success and failure and the difference between incremental improvement and the need for substantive change.

The Family Business

This approach lacks accountability, although there is a calling. In this type of organization, only close family members hold leadership positions, and the ministry is usually wholly dependent on outside funding.

Money-centric

These types of organizations have strategies, policies, and programs that exist because "it's where the money is." In the early 1990s, as micro-enterprise loan funds developed, many small and large missions found that their givers were more receptive to these types of perceived sustainable solutions for the poor than their core activities. The danger, of course, is that you must make payroll to stay in business. This mindset may lead to mission creep into areas where ministries aren't competent, weren't called to, or don't offer an appropriate response to the long-term needs of the beneficiaries. Sticking with a proven calling and ministry and doing proper fundraising are the antidotes.

Overdependence

This involves relying on a single funding source or on a single class of funds, such as foundations or a small circle of donors. It's a violation of the optimal funding pyramid.

Givers and investors must be able to discern if any of these conditions exist within a ministry under consideration for a gift. However, I've never encountered a ministry that's totally free of *all* these conditions. Ministries, after all, are led by human beings who are still somewhere on the road to perfection. The particular challenges a ministry faces in getting its work done may make things look very messy. Note that I'm not dealing here with issues of malfeasance or fraud, which are often masked by financial success and the ability to shroud sinful behavior from scrutiny.

Some Basic Questions

As a coach to mission leaders, I begin by simply asking standard questions, like a doctor does when he pokes you somewhere and asks, "Does this hurt?"

My version of the question is this: How much money do you need? This may seem crass or even overly personal. But when you work in philanthropy or organizational coaching, the conversation often circles back to some form of this opening question.

It's one of my favorite questions, because I'm almost always amazed at how many leaders are stumped for a coherent answer. The main reason is that they're often considering only the shortfall of their budget or what they perceive as their own personal responsibility. This gives me a chance to state the obvious: that no matter how much it takes to run the ministry, *it's all your responsibility as the leader*. The leader is responsible for the whole budget—every single penny, no matter who's doing the fundraising or where the revenue comes from.

The leader's job is to make sure everyone else can do theirs. And at the end of the day, the issue holding the leader back may well be money. Or so it may seem. You can learn a lot about leaders by observing their views about money: how they get it, spend it, and trust God for it.

Obviously, it's not easy to be the boss. In fact, in many ways, it's the toughest job in any organization. To follow the example of Jesus—to empty yourself in order to fill up everyone else—is as hard a task as there is.

"It's lonely at the top," so the saying goes, but this is true only if you're a leader who doesn't have a prayer life and doesn't have the know-how or desire to build a team. The trap is to set yourself apart so much that singularity becomes a model of leadership.

Yes, it's true, as the leader, you alone may have to shoulder some hard, ultimate decisions—such as letting a key staff member go, cutting a program with many supporters, weighing between competing factions of advisors, or (most commonly) having to make a critical decision with incomplete information.

However, these and other challenges are more manageable and easier to navigate when the hard work of achieving a balanced accountability structure has been taken on.

In my role, further digging usually leads me to look closer at the executive-board relationship and to ask: "Are all your board members giving?"

The Board's Job

If you lead a ministry, sometime in your career you'll likely encounter a board that wields power without providing the counterpart of covering, aka "we've got your back."

In light of this, I developed a simple job description checklist for board members that helps me understand what's going on and what might need correcting in an organization's structure.

Whether serving on a board for a small local ministry or for a large international ministry, all board members serving in ministry should possess the following attributes:

Figure 6

BOARD MEMBERS JOB DESCRIPTION

- Must have a love for the work of the ministry, not just a love for the person running the ministry.
- Must love the purpose of the organization.
- Must be personal givers to the ministry. They have money to give and to pay their own way to board meetings and to travel on behalf of the ministry.

- Must be in the inner circle of the orbit, not on the fringe of the circle.
- Must have influence or affluence.
- Must be elders or of elder qualities, man or woman.
- Spouse must be in 100 percent agreement.
- All board members are friends, advocates, and advisors. However, one does not have to be a board member to be a friend, advocate, or advisor.

When the Board Is Unhealthy

To emphasize the importance of the board's function in an organization, here's a list of unhealthy characteristics in boards to watch for:

Somebody "jumped" the orbit or was "promoted" to the board because of a false hope or false need. He or she didn't move through the various layers of incrementally deeper involvement, such as going from a friend who has made multiple gifts and who regularly interacts with the mission to becoming an advisor who has displayed an intimate knowledge of and interest in the work and who can be counted on to be thoughtfully useful. Instead, someone is put in the center of things with little or no track record with the mission. This type of person can be, and usually is, a dangerous addition to the leadership structure, bringing change for change's sake because the mission is desperate for a turnaround.

God's will is sublimated to human will as merely good ideas predominate over God-given ideas and vision. An example (one that's related also to the above point) is when someone who isn't an "elder"—and who's lacking in proven, spiritual discernment—immediately jumps in with ideas and notions for change without having a requisite background in the mission's issues and challenges . . . or, even more damaging, doesn't have sufficient experience in his faith walk to sit in judgment of the mission's operating vision and strategies. This doesn't mean God won't use outsiders or outside-the-box thinking to shake up hidebound structures and policies. He will, and He does—and often it's His preferred way of getting our attention. However, discernment is essential, and maturity in the believers serving in accountability structures is preferred. It's hard work to know when to seize an opportunity, pursue a new goal, or just say no. In addition, God will allow missions that glorify man and dishonor Him to be beset with satanic attack or with adulation (which is just as dangerous).

Board members can be distracted if their spouse isn't 100 percent in agreement with how much time, money, and energy is being expended on behalf of the mission. A distracted board member who isn't all-in on the job will be a drag on the mission's progress.

A lack of synergy can cause a distance between the executive and the board. This can lead to an out-of-balance wobble and also create friction, thus impeding the mission's progress.

These things often happen when boards assume operational responsibility under the belief that they can micromanage a mission out of trouble or into a growth spurt, or when a board shrugs off responsibility because of a lack of deep love for the organization. Other related factors include: board members being spread too thin, serving out of some need for perceived prestige, or serving because of friendship or assignment, as when a member fills a spot on a mission board only because they represent a constituency.

Even though disagreements are and should be a normal part of board deliberations, consensus—joyfully achieved as a coming together of minds—needs to be the goal of all decision-making. The hard work of a board is to seek such consensus even if it means delaying decisions, resignations, and other proper partings of ways.

Confusion must be studied and dealt with, since it's folly to believe Satan won't serve up confusion to discourage effective ministry.

Healthy Boards
When board health is present, I find the board members were recruited from the advisor level of the orbit, not having jumped the concentric rings of the orbit, but having proven over time their love for the organization and not just its purpose.

Other indicators of health:

There's clear distinction between policy and vision. Vision is expressed from the executive and tested by the board, which establishes policy. The staff implements the work.

The board understands its responsibility in the critical aspects of covering the executive, representing the stakeholders, and ensuring fidelity to the ministry's calling.

New blood is being injected into the board on a regular basis, and transition planning for the founder and contingency planning for current executives are in place.

Institutional memory is a valued asset. Longevity of well-performing staff is rewarded, and the deep smarts of an organization are memorialized in operating principles, values, and a proper respect for history that's balanced with the need for innovation as well as incremental improvement.

The achievement of planned outcomes is celebrated. A realistically run ministry also celebrates sincere effort even if, due to unanticipated challenges, the planned outcome wasn't achieved. Retreats and bonding exercises are also hallmarks of successful ministries, offering time together for resting in God and for contemplation.

Board members have both influence and affluence. These two things must be offered to the mission in exchange for the authority the board members hold. This is how prominent elders—both men and women—give back to the wider community for the success they've been graced with. (Influence means even if they lack the ability themselves to do significant grants, they have a proven ability to influence others to give.)

Failure is studied for the lesson to be gained. Careful evaluation and planning is undertaken before risky mergers and the like are undertaken.

Facing into the truth is valued, even when it is difficult. Knowing and acting on the truth can lead to the most uncomfortable actions you may ever have to take. God is love, and if your faith in Him is rooted and growing, there's nothing you can't face in either your personal or your mission's life.

Introspection—a healthy self-awareness—is always present. This is one of the key reasons vision must come from the executive and be confirmed and tested by the accountability structure. A good executive sees and discerns reality on a daily basis and accounts for it.

Feedback loops—with set points of "plan," "do," "measure," and "change"—are continuous in every major program or department as a way of avoiding micromanagement and staying aware of challenges and opportunities. Feedback loops are useful ways to organize a staff meeting. Each loop with a program name on it needs to have a designated individual responsible for it—even if the staff is small, and one person may have responsibility for multiple loops.

Development reviews are instituted as a regular practice, separate from annual performance reviews. The point of development reviews is to make sure the board and the mission executive are on the same page and working toward fixing problems, not sweeping them under the rug. This is true also of supervisors working with people who directly report to them. Most missions I've observed don't do development reviews, to their detriment. A development review begins with a comparison of two written job descriptions—the one perceived to be in place by the employer and the real description of what someone is actually doing on a daily basis. This comparison process clears up assumptions and miscommunication. Next comes a review of what's gone right and what has been achieved from both points of view, followed by a similar analysis of what could have gone better. This both affirms the individual and points out—in the least threatening way—where improvement is needed. The last part of the review addresses barriers to improvement and a lasting plan to overcome whatever difficulties or challenges exist. These reviews differ from annual performance reviews, which should be conducted six months apart from the development review.

Success is questioned. While success is preferred to failure, organizations that don't question their success are inevitably setting themselves up for failure. Constituencies, including funders, gravitate toward successful programs, so questioning such success can bring a gut-churning sensation. To rock the boat is counter-intuitive. While incremental improvement is always sought, there's a prudent time in all organizations, programs, and procedures to pause and evaluate where things stand. Often, because of success, there'll be a change in the dynamics of the ills you're seeking to correct, bringing a new dynamic to bear. Knowing how to cope with this change is valuable. Further study on this should be required of all executives and boards, if for no other reason, to understand that change in the midst of success will produce chaos that must be embraced as the ministry experiences the unforeseen elements that always accompany disruption.[1] Lastly, it's important not to relax for long with any idea that something is "good enough"—because sooner than later, it won't be.

The organization reviews its margins, because often the best ideas can be found beyond the boundaries of normative practice. People have died over this type of healthy review; just look at the Reformation. The church throughout its history has consistently moved boundaries in or out as new ideas challenged orthodoxy. For example, the gnostic heresies were kept out, whereas vernacular worship was included. The challenges may not be quite so dramatic in your organization, but resisting change that is called for can prove costly to your health.

When planning, the long view is taken, but objectives are implemented in short, deliberate steps.[2]

Restoring the Board's Good Health

When a board shows signs of sickness, there are ways back to good health:

1. Go to war on the attitude that efficiency trumps effectiveness.

I've encountered a dangerous shibboleth over the years—that investors will be attracted to efficiency. It isn't true. More critical than efficiency is *what* will be accomplished . . . and the effort put in, no matter the obstacles. Efficiency must be a given and strived for in ministry but only in service to effectiveness.

I focus on well-run organizations that are actually getting something done. As mentioned earlier, figuring out the difference between programmatic costs and administrative costs is more than a challenge. In the end, the expenses are all administrative in nature. The money buys stuff, pays salaries, rents apartments, and builds or digs wells. Somebody's being paid even if you have a self-funded volunteer (they get their food somewhere).

2. Prune for a better harvest.

God values people, but we devalue them when we keep them in jobs they aren't suited for. (Development reviews can help identify this.) This isn't an excuse to fire; it's the opposite. In most cases, people who aren't succeeding in their work have not been properly developed, or the recruiting process wasn't given sufficient time or energy. With "pruning," the energy of the organization is directed to producing the best fruit, not the most.

3. Focus on the board-executive relationship.

This is a major indicator of organizational health, and that's especially true in how the board chair works with an executive committee (if it exists). Wisdom, prudence, and time are some of the most important attributes a board chair must exhibit. The board chair and the executive should work assiduously so as to not let there be any daylight between them.

The Tension Triangle

Finally, well-run organizations operate best within a Tension Triangle.

Figure 7

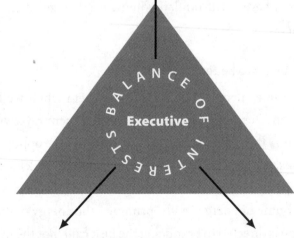

TENSION TRIANGLE

Stakeholders / Investors

Executive

BALANCE OF INTERESTS

Beneficiaries / Customers   **Staff / Employees**

I learned about this concept from my boss, Peter Ochs, coprincipal of First Fruit and a successful developer. He uses the Tension Triangle to explain the natural tensions between owners, customers, and employees.

Owners want profits. Customers want low prices and high quality. Employees want good pay for a day's work. As Peter explains it, a properly run business creates a balance between these seemingly competitive interests. Owners get reasonable profits, which are necessary for the health of the business and to create a fair reward for their risks taken; customers get a good quality product and appropriate pricing, so the business can stay competitive but outshine its competition; and employees feel valued and rewarded for their efforts.

The executive of the organization must artfully achieve these balancing interests by managing *up* to the investors and other stakeholders, managing *down* to the employees, and managing *out* to the customers.

When a business is out of balance, as Peter sees it, the prospect for failure and being overtaken by competition is inevitable. When I learned this, I saw its implication for the executive's role in a nonprofit where the stakeholders are the board and givers, the employees are the staff and missionaries, and the customers are the beneficiaries of the loving acts of the mission.

When these roles on the triangle get out of balance—employees might be overpaid, donors are program drivers, or everything is sacrificed for the beneficiary—leaders will lose sight of proper management.

Loving others well is a great way to start figuring all this out while tackling the three tasks for financial growth in a mission. In the final three chapters, we'll look at each one separately. Three elements make up the overarching process of mission fundraising: discovery, acquisition, and nurturing. These are separate but completely interrelated efforts—each with a distinct set of tasks, all of equal importance and requiring equal effort.

When money goes on mission

... it comes with a joyful offering of trust and is met with a joyful offering of accountability.

13

DISCOVERY

Finding Those Who May Join Your Work

WHEN WE GIVE, this joyful act helps us feel alive and connected with the whole body of Christ. Until you give, you may not know the fullness of this expression of worship. But those who give do know, and they keep their eyes open for opportunities to give more.

The task of *discovery* means getting in front of as many potential givers as you can, appropriately announcing your purpose, and seeing who God may be calling to invest with you in the opportunity you're presenting.

To understand the work of discovery, it is important to map out your funding universe. This is especially critical for autochthonous funding initiatives as their default is, most often, to include the West because it appears that the largest gifts could, or should, come from there.

Think first of who your funders should be; i.e. international ministries should have an international donor base, local ministries, a local base, etc. Often the universe expands with work, but if you go for the big easy grants first, like buying lottery tickets, however tempting, you may never establish a sustained base of support.

It's not complicated—but it might take some creativity. Discovering where potential investors in your mission exist occurs in five basic ways, most anywhere in the world: love gifts, events, direct response, speaking, and networking.

Love Gifts

Those of us who've worked in missions know about *love gifts*. It's when the mission is discovered first by the giver, rather than vice versa. The money is given without any effort on the ministry's part, and it's a surprise. Often when churches or small groups take up special offerings for a missionary or mission, they call it a love gift; but what I'm referring to are gifts that show up out of the blue. If your ministry is well known, people can find you when they feel motivated to give to your purpose.

A few years ago, I had the privilege of doing some fundraising coaching with the leadership team of a large Bible translation ministry. They had an avalanche of these kind of love gifts, and they also received considerable funding from people leaving them money and real assets in their wills.

Every ministry leader I've ever talked with about this has experienced this particular grace of God—often when it was needed most. At the Rescue Mission, the stories about the frozen steaks and the box of gold highlighted such unexpected gifts. At the time, we were listed in the phone book and were known to be feeding the homeless. Today, a ministry would most likely be found on the web or through social media. I've learned that although you can't plan on love gifts, you can count on God to provide them. When working in Christian missions, expect the unexpected.

Even if you don't know the origin of the gift, it does give you a contact name to add to your list of givers, and names are critical when nurturing relationships with givers as we'll see in the last chapter.

Events

Events are another area where unexpected gifts are given. There's no end to the creative experiences missions have come up with to get their message in front of potential givers. There's also no end to the frustration, exhilaration, and downright disappointment associated with the exhausting work of planning and executing events.

Banquets are often the first type of event that comes to mind. They've been used as an inducement to participation in something or other since time immemorial. Why not? Who doesn't enjoy a meal with friends? Or that's the idea, at least, behind most banquets.

My wife and I recently received an invitation from a ministry to "purchase a table" for $350. The ministry hopes that we'll invite eight friends (who don't know about the mission) to a meal of rubbery chicken and overlong speeches with a musical interlude, followed by a baffling request for funds.

In this instance, the ministry that invited my wife and me has been important in our daughter's life. We want to support this ministry, but the banquet site is more than a day's drive from where we live, and we don't have that many friends who'd be interested in going. If we buy a table, how will we fill the seats? So, on the one hand, the answer from us should be no. However, I can't stand the thought of this wonderful ministry putting out a tremendous amount of effort to slaughter who knows how many sacrificial chickens, only to have an empty hall when the night of the event occurs. I've experienced that, and there's no joy when you go to bed on a night like that.

Whatever money banquets raise, they are unparalleled at being a sort of family event. At the Rescue Mission, we invited pastors from our volunteers' churches to be our evening speakers. In every case, they brought in significant investors and new friends to the work. Our fundraising appeal was simple as well. We used the banquet as a graduation exercise for our New Life program, where former lost souls from the streets gave their testimonies of how Jesus had changed their lives and set them on a new path to experiencing the abundance of God's kingdom. There was never a dry eye in the house, and with good reason. The testimonies were real and raw. They spoke of the love God has for us and how that love changes lives.

Other popular fundraising events include: golf tournaments, 5k runs, silent auctions, festivals, and mission weekends.

When putting on events to raise money for your ministry, be careful of the amount of effort required. You must carefully balance that against the rewards.

Or not.

During my early time at the Rescue Mission, I once devoted my entire $5,000 marketing budget to renting the large convention hall in our county, and I invited Keith Green, a popular Christian singer at the time, to present a free concert. I thought this was God's idea but couldn't be certain.

Before the concert, I remember being handed a little pouch

from one of the assistant managers at our bank; I hoped to fill that pouch with the proceeds, and I told the assistant manager I'd be back to open a large savings account. From the look he gave me, I'm pretty sure he wasn't convinced.

But I was. I just didn't know what I didn't know, and I didn't do a good job of anticipating what happened next.

I hadn't marketed the event outside our monthly mailing. I thought a few hundred people would show up at most. I'd invited a local church to send over their ushers to help manage the crowd and to take up the offering. They sent five people. When I arrived in the late afternoon at the convention center, I had to fight my way through a throng of thousands. Some had arrived early in busloads from churches, some from more than 100 miles away. The police came, trying to manage the crowd; they were quite upset with me when nearby freeway off-ramps backed up.

The crowd was mostly young people. Even my future wife (who I didn't know at the time) was there. It was clear we were going to fill the hall's seven thousand seats, and we'd be turning away a significant number of others as well. (The police later estimated that several thousand were turned away.) I was stunned and completely unprepared.

I sent someone to beg a local Kentucky Fried Chicken restaurant to give us sixty cardboard buckets so we could take up the offering. When the buckets arrived, I literally prayed and handed them out to volunteer teenagers I didn't know, hoping they would all bring the buckets back. The few ushers from the church organized this crew. I went on stage and introduced Keith. With just his voice and piano and one spotlight, he held

the audience enthralled in worship for nearly three hours. Keith
directed the taking of the offering during the concert. Afterward,
down in the convention center's basement, all the buckets were
accounted for, each brimming with loose change and dollar
bills—all that the young people in attendance could afford and
had in their pockets.

I had to borrow twelve cardboard boxes from the convention
center staff to take the money home with me, since we had no
time to count the money there. I loaded my car with the boxes,
took them to my apartment, and put my mattress on top of
them. I literally slept on the proceeds. The concert was on Friday
night; I didn't leave my apartment until Monday morning, when
I drove the boxes to the mission's office, and we began to count.
Two days later, we had a tally of nearly $37,000 in nickels, dimes,
pennies, and dollar bills.

I opened that new savings account. And the Rescue Mission never looked back. Those young people—our living
stones—had put us on the map, and our growth was steadily up
from there.

It doesn't take much.

Remember the Romanian leader who saw a fancy silent auction in the United States, returned home to try the same idea,
and his ministry was launched by the donation of a used pair
of gym socks? Undeterred, he used the event to launch a local
fundraising effort for the mission which today not only totally
funds its own work, but has sent several offerings to other nations, including Egypt, so they could start their own program.

I wish I could say there was a successful formula here—there
isn't. Just do your best to honor God.

Direct Response

Missions familiar with direct response efforts know that this method involves quite a bit of math—from simple arithmetic to sophisticated formulas used by multi-million-dollar operations. However, in concept it's not complicated. Direct response means directly asking for a gift, usually through advertising—by mail, phone calls, electronic means of various sorts, and even Santa Clauses ringing bells on a street corner. (If you don't know this or haven't been in the United States at Christmastime, Google it.) So, where does the math come in?

Some think direct response fundraising, like any form of advertising, is simple: expose your work to a thousand people, and if thirty respond to your offer, you'll gain them as new givers and perhaps also fund the campaign that found them.

For simplicity's sake, let's say the 1,000 direct response pieces you sent cost $1,000 to prepare and mail, and the average gift received was $25. You would need forty people to respond just to pay the cost of the mailing, or four percent of the cohort you sent the appeal to. The actual average is much lower—normally, in my experience, it's about two percent.

So what makes it worth the effort and expense? Usually a new giver acquired in this manner will give more in response to future mailings and may well stay with the mission over an extended period of time. This makes direct response viable, because otherwise, as in the example above, the cost of fundraising would be one hundred percent, with no money going to the work of the mission itself.

As the size and complexity of the campaign grows, statistical analysis and formula applications can help the mission to segment its donor base and respect those givers with a knowledge-based approach. But be aware that these same tools have been used by scoundrels for scams, as we see almost daily in news accounts of the misuse of social media data. A discerning leader must learn to sift the wheat from the chaff when launching such a program and be certain that God has deemed this to be an appropriate way to raise funds.

Direct response advertising is far and away the single largest source of revenue for many large, well-respected, well-managed US missions, particularly those involved in relief and development work. More importantly, it's an effective method for allowing givers of limited means to make small gifts as a significant way to participate in mission. We see this especially as younger givers around the world prefer to donate through their smartphones and other internet-based avenues.

Because direct response advertising can be used for good or evil intents, a giver's ability to discern the character of the mission's leaders, and whether they're trustworthy, becomes paramount. In the United States, a good place to start for understanding this is to see if the ministry has achieved approval from the ECFA[1] to use its seal on their mailings and other forms of solicitation. Internationally, efforts are underway to establish ECFA-type functions in India, Philippines, Korea, and East Africa.

Many missionaries and mission agencies think direct response work means emailing occasional reports and perhaps snail-mailing out a trifold newsletter once a quarter or so. These practices arise out of an innate desire to be courteous—to not want to impose or be a bother, but also to stay in touch with supporters. These communications typically come with the mission's hope of encouraging prayer and further giving, again without being perceived as a bother. An even more passive approach in recent times has meant putting a "Donate Here" button on a website, Facebook page, or other social media outreach. However, for the purpose of bringing in funds, these practices usually yield dismal results.

SPECIFICALLY ASKING SOMEONE TO JOIN YOU FINANCIALLY ON YOUR JOURNEY IS HOW MOST FUNDS GET RAISED.

Fundraising raises money, and specifically asking someone to join you financially on your journey is how most funds get raised. But, presenting simple information is a notoriously poor way of raising funds. Those who practice it as a fundraising technique are working off the assumption that once someone is informed about a problem, they'll make the leap to understanding how your ideas are the solution. It seems logical: explain the need, show how you're working on it, and givers will flock to you without you having to go through the unpleasant task of asking them directly for funds.

There are several problems with this assumption. First, people generally don't make that leap. Second, you may be preaching to the choir. What if the only people reading your materials are people who are already deeply engaged with you? Furthermore, what if your newsletters, or even your appeal letters, never get read by new potential investors? They quickly hit the delete button on your emails or drop your unopened envelopes into the kitchen trash. You may consider your writings to be sacred—as indeed they are, since they showcase a sacred activity—but few other people will. If a newsletter, appeal letter, or "Donate Here" button works at all to bring in any new investors, it's only because God has helped an individual sort through the noise of everyday life to find you.

One last thought on numbers: when I mentioned that out of a mailing of a thousand appeal letters, perhaps twenty responses would be tallied (which is about average for a successful letter), that was for a mailing to an active in-house donor list. However, when sending appeals to lists that have been rented or borrowed, successful numbers will usually be much less—perhaps just one in a hundred, or even less. You'd be correct in assuming that sending 10,000 letters will likely produce only 100 to 300 responses.

I believe in God's economy. He views the math quite differently. Before God, we've all been encouraged to be generous and to give what we're persuaded in our hearts to give. Paul mentions this, of course, in his second letter to the Corinthians, but God Himself says the same thing, as recorded in Exodus 25:1–2, "The Lord said to Moses, 'Tell the Israelites to bring me an offering. You are to receive the offering for me from everyone whose heart prompts them to give.'"

For all human problems—from loneliness, to running for your life to escape a war-torn country, to all the heartfelt sobs of the least, the last, and the lost, to the need for health and wellness—God wants His people to be His hands reaching out to help. That's what He's instructed us to do; amazingly, the Creator of the universe has chosen *us* to be His instruments of mercy (Matt. 25:31–40). As individuals, none of us is called to meet

all the needs. However, every cry for help needs *someone* to respond—for the harvest is great, and the workers are few.

So, if you're reaching out to a group of 10,000 potential
givers, perhaps God is nudging only a few to be interested in
your particular work—but He wants all 10,000 to be involved
somewhere. So, don't fret about who's *not* responding; be focused
on who *is*.

Remember, Paul didn't drop indirect hints to the Greeks
that they take up an offering for the Jews in Jerusalem. He asked
them directly, and he gave them plenty of good reasons why they
should be generous. Do the same—and do it consistently. Let
the people you're hoping to reach know exactly how you'll use
their money to fulfill a purpose they're attracted to. And send the
appeal letters out monthly; don't think you're being bothersome
or disrespectful of people's privacy. Givers will let you know if
you're bothering them; they'll unsubscribe, or ask to be taken off
your list, or simply not respond over a long period of time. In any
case, trust that you'll get the hint.

Social media's many platforms are now coming to domi-
nate all forms of direct response advertising. Just like with all
of media, it won't work if the intended responders are directed
to a generic offer which doesn't specifically tell them how to be
involved or doesn't give them a context for their gift. But, when
done right, social media and your web presence, depending on
the adoption rate of web-based services in any particular country, can become a critical quarry for living stone donations.

Be aware of your proclivities regarding fundraising, and
don't hide your funding needs behind storytelling, education, or
prayer requests. *Let your needs be known.* Let your prayer request

be just that. When telling a story, make it about God and what He's up to, and how you're fortunate to be along for the ride.

Speaking

Speaking is the least understood method of fundraising, but perhaps the most effective way of discovering new potential givers. Most speaking engagements are for this purpose of discovery; the actual *acquisition* of people to become investors is another, separate task. Speaking is also the easiest discovery method to do—and the easiest to mess up. I believe I've experienced all kinds of messing up when it comes to public speaking, including going too long and wandering off-point (what my dear wife refers to as "chicken walking" when I do it).

I've even made the mistake of not speaking long enough. It happened on a Sunday morning in Buenos Aires when I was on a First Fruit fact-finding trip with my wife and one of our board members. We were in a large Brethren church of perhaps more than a thousand people, and the pastor had set the three of us on the platform to his right. He'd told me beforehand that he'd be asking me to "bring a word of greeting." So, when he called on me, I stood up and said, "Hi, I'm Rob Martin." I introduced my wife and the board member who was with us, then quickly concluded by letting everyone know we were from California. And then I sat down.

The response was a stunned silence, which for the life of me I couldn't fathom. I wasn't fundraising that day, and I thought I'd done well in not taking advantage of this man's pulpit.

After an awkward few moments, the pastor got up and carried on with the service. Only later did I learn that in that setting, to "bring a word of greeting" means giving a scriptural message of a few minutes or more. I haven't been surprised by that one again.

If you're leading a ministry, you'll be called on at times to speak. Before I learned much about fundraising, all I knew to do was to talk to people—as many as I could. I estimate that over a four-year period I spoke more than two hundred times to various groups—from missions committees to church congregations both large and small on Sunday nights and Sunday mornings. I spoke at Wednesday night potlucks, Saturday morning men's breakfasts—and once, even a ladies-only church garden club. I spoke anywhere and everywhere I could. I didn't know how to say no to a speaking engagement, so I asked God not to bring me any request that He didn't want me to take.

The invitations came directly from those who were volunteering for the work. Between our nightly services and other volunteer work experiences we offered, we had dozens of churches engaged with us at any one time. We were managing thousands of volunteer hours.

Whether your ministry is large or small, if you can witness to Jesus and to the power of the cross, you'll be heard. But there are a few guidelines to keep in mind.

First, a common error is to think that churches, as a regular practice, give money out of their operating budgets. They don't. If they have a missions budget, it's probably spoken for, and you'll need an advocate to invite you into their process. What you want from a church is the trust of the pastor. This is something to be prized and treated with deep respect. If the pastor endorses you, and you make it clear you don't want to divert money from church programs, then that pastor's endorsement will open up members of the congregation who are drawn to your purpose to become your givers. This is the long and short of why you should speak.

All righteous missions have great stories. You'll have stories to tell about the power to change lives and bring about redemption and reconciliation. You'll have stories of triumph, and stories revealing passion for what God has called you to. Your job will be to bless whoever you're in front of with these stories in some coherent format. Tell your stories so that the purpose of what you do shines through.

TELL YOUR STORIES SO THAT THE PURPOSE OF WHAT YOU DO SHINES THROUGH.

Some churches you speak at will take up offerings, some will not. But if a few people walk away with your brochure or your information—or, even, if not—God will have honored your time, for if you're faithful to His word, it never comes back void.

Networking

In the orbit figure we looked at in the last chapter, the innermost rings include advocates, advisors, and (at the center) the leader and board members. This is where *connecting* occurs. The best connections will come from these givers.

First, two warnings:

When connecting, being able to handle the word *no* becomes a critical skill. You've got to learn not to take that rejection personally. No matter how dire the circumstances of the need you're addressing—or the needs of your mission to address it— the only investors you want are those whom God has called to your work, those who connect with your purpose, and who want to thankfully participate in seeing it fulfilled.

Second, it's hard work. This is the never-ending quest of a leader. Remember, the leader's job is to make sure everyone else in the organization can do his or her work.

Begin with time management. You must give real time— every day—to the task of connecting. If you have people (such as development officers) designated to help you in this, don't think of it as your passport for ignoring the task yourself. It just means you have to work harder because you now have a team to lead in finding funds for your ministry, which means you have to be available to your team.

Whether the person you meet with is the matriarch of the Rockefeller family in a tower that carries her name or a mechanic running a business out of his garage (both of whom I've met), your approach should be the same: respectful and appropriate to the circumstances. It might require a full-blown written proposal with financials, endorsements, and ministry reports. It might mean wearing a suit and flying across the country. Or if it's someone like the backyard mechanic, he may just want to look you in the eye and judge for himself if he can trust you. One size doesn't fit all when it comes to connecting. Every single meeting will be different; each will require you to prepare appropriately.

But don't despair. This is God-honoring work. In fundraising, yours is the privilege of being a part of a great adventure.

HALLELUJAH!

Back when I didn't have to worry about the decor of where I hung out, my stepbrother Tim painted that word in huge block letters across the back wall of my office at the Mission. I needed to remember that God inhabits our praises. As my church pastor, Luis Sanchez, likes to say, "We worship Him for who He is, and praise Him for what He does."

It's easy to despair in the hard work of managing an organization that's accomplishing anything useful. You can get lost in the minutia of management and easily lose sight of what's important when you're buried in paper.

In my early days, when preparing the financials of the Rescue Mission, I often felt either hair-pulling anxiety or a bout of deadly boredom. Noticing this, Lewis admonished me to get out of my office, go out to the waiting area of the Mission, find the nastiest drunk person—and hug him.

This is still good advice. When you get buried in the minutia of making sure everyone else can do their job, then get up and throw off the shackles of your smartphone, your spreadsheets, unfinished proposals, and emails demanding immediate response that don't really need it. Go and get directly involved with the ultimate loving action of your mission, if even for only a moment. Then get back to work.

Hallelujah!

When money goes on mission

Discovery is learning who and where your potential partners are. For both givers and receivers, when money goes on mission, it moves beyond a transaction and begins the process of transformational relationship between these partners.

14

ACQUISITION

Communicating to Raise and Give Money

WHEN I BEGAN working in international mission philanthropy, I realized how little I really knew about how people come
to faith in settings outside the United States.

When you do this kind of work, the ability to visualize how
complex and unfamiliar things function is a handy skill to develop. It's tough to feel comfortable recommending something
to be funded if you don't clearly comprehend what you're being
asked to fund.

Most proposals aren't written lyrically and probably
shouldn't be, but without descriptive nuance, mere words con-
strained in length on paper can struggle to convey the understanding of strategic concepts which are often very involved.
What needs to be clear is the simple idea: the ultimate loving
action of the gospel and the hope that undergirds it all.

In my first years of working at First Fruit, when I prepared
for a board meeting I developed a habit of setting aside a specific time alone in my office with all the proposal ideas from our
prospective grantees listed on a large whiteboard behind my
desk. It was crunch time, and I had to choose which proposals I

would put into our book of recommendations. I considered each of them and tried to picture the loving action of the gospel that would eventually be accomplished if the grant would succeed in helping the grantee achieve his or her purpose. I was working off the idea that most mission comes down to a Christian doing something loving for another person. It might be telling someone about the love of Jesus and hoping to bring that person into a relationship with Him. Or it could merely be responding to someone in need.

This visualization exercise wasn't always easy. Often, knowledge gaps exist between the potential giver and the ultimate loving action of the gospel in a ministry. Knowledge gaps occur especially in large organizations or associations where there are many levels of management or networks that play a role in the processes or strategies that ultimately result in the loving actions of the gospel.

Acquisition—the theme of this chapter—is essentially about helping to bring a deeper level of understanding to those who are called to join you on your journey—your givers, investors, board members, volunteers, and staff—all from the universe God has assigned for your ministry. You help them understand your loving actions. You do this by communicating your story in a way that eliminates knowledge gaps, and by writing three specific kinds of documents: white papers, letters of inquiry, and proposals.

The outer ring of the funding orbit is known as Acquaintance (see Figure 2, chapter 12). As you move in the orbit from discovery to acquisition, your first givers will be acquaintances. What follows are the methods to make that happen.

CLOSING THE KNOWLEDGE GAPS

Just like the work of discovering givers discussed in the previous chapter—and just like the task of nurturing that we'll explore in the next—acquisition is hard work.

Early in my time with First Fruit, we made grants to help underwrite some of the formative meetings of what has become known as the North African Partnership. The grants were for the costs associated with gathering into one room representatives of the many ministries working for the evangelization of North Africa, to see what synergies could happen as they explored working together. In regard to their efforts, I searched to find the loving action of the gospel—that single loving act at the farthest extension of their work. I found it helpful to ask a primary question like this: "What happens on Tuesday when a missionary working alone in a Cairo suburb starts his day?"

Based on my visits in the field and my observations and conversations during partnership meetings, I'd learned that one of this missionary's key loving actions of the gospel was to invite a Muslim seeker to tea. The missionary inviting the seeker could have been trained as a church volunteer, as a mission staff member, or as a full-time, self-supported worker. The Muslim seeker, perhaps while channel-surfing a satellite feed on his TV, might have stumbled onto a broadcast of a Bible study ostensibly meant for Christians. Drawn to the message out of curiosity, he responded with his cell phone to the "I want to know Jesus" button on the broadcaster's website. The collected information was then conveyed to workers in the field, one of whom in turn invited the seeker to tea. All this had the potential, over several months, of a seeker accepting an invitation to a home fellowship and then coming to faith.

I learned that this simple act of having tea came about because of the working together of a complex array of organizations, strategies, and sacrificial outreach, all of which existed to accomplish a specific purpose. In this grant's case, all we did was help fund the meeting where the broadcasters, call centers, scriptwriters, web designers, missionary training ministries, Bible translation agencies, Middle Eastern churches and seminaries, and on-the-ground missions teams came together to work out how to encourage the simple loving action of taking someone to tea.

The exercise I went through in my office—imagining the eventual loving actions of the gospel in each of the proposals I was deliberating—gave me the necessary insight to be able to help my foundation's board of directors understand the purpose of each of the proposals they were to consider. Understanding this is important in the development of resources because those who'll be attracted to joining you on your journey will need to understand the context of the actions they'll be taking as a volunteer, staff member, or investor. They'll need to understand how their role is connected to the ultimate loving action of the gospel, no matter what part of the overall task your ministry is engaged in. When you're able to do this, you're closing the natural-occurring knowledge gaps that exist between you, your work, and those you're sharing your story with, so that they'll join in your journey.

In this example of the North African Partnership, it could be easy to get stumped trying to see through all the various strategies and complex challenges that lead to the simple act of meeting someone for tea. So, the loving action had to be made clear and interesting for those who wanted to know more before they invested time, energy, or money. Because I'd enjoyed the privilege of traveling and doing site visits with some of those involved in the North African Partnership, my visualization exercise was pretty much on-point.

This bears repeating. *It's important for people who join you on your journey to know and understand the ultimate loving actions of your ministry*, so they won't lose interest.

Closing knowledge gaps takes away the confusion and mystery in mission messaging. There's no simpler way to acquire an investor from your potential universe—someone who has turned his or her attention toward you—than to close those knowledge gaps. So, as you prepare your materials for those you want to join you on your journey, close the gaps for them, even if they don't ask you to.

Closing the gaps also includes truthfully telling your actual story. In that example of the missionary in a Cairo suburb on a Tuesday morning, extrapolated from a real story, many of the Muslim people the missionary might have contacted would be wary and untrusting; hence, the emphasis was on nothing more than having tea. And of course, many of these invitations were turned down. The missionary spent hours in prayer for each of his contacts. The work was slow, and hardly ever followed a neat and simple pattern—and that's the point. The truth in that Cairo suburb is no different than the truth in the neighborhood of the giver.

Try to imagine how many people you might lead to the Lord today. Rev. Lewis Whitehead used to consider his day a failure if he hadn't led somebody to the Lord by lunchtime—and even then, he wasn't satisfied. He was a persuasive man. He wanted to make sure you not only had prayed the sinner's prayer, but also had begun immediately to become discipled. Each day was the same for him, even as he lay dying in the hospital. One morning I came into his office and found my mother with Lewis, kneeling in prayer and accepting Christ. She was one tough nut to crack—yet there she was in her mid-fifties, praying the sinner's prayer. Years later when she died, still tough as nails, her final words were these, "I know Jesus loves me, and I love Him. I love you, and I'm ready to die."

I've never come close to Lewis's energy in saving lives, but whether in the streets of Cairo or Santa Ana, the loving actions I've observed are pretty similar. Meanwhile, the processes for achieving these loving actions are often quite varied.

The Complexity of Knowledge Gaps

Besides the sheer challenge of grasping what's going on in a particular grant, other knowledge gaps are problematic, not just for givers and investors, but for various layers of management.

In a large organization where there may be multiple mission stations, preaching points, clinics, campuses, or far-flung offices, there are many more knowledge gaps to overcome. For example, I can think of a supervisor in a church-planting mission in South Asia who has multiple preaching points spread across enough terrain that he needs overnight stays to visit them all. At each of the preaching points, a church planter reports to the line supervisor who has several home groups or small house churches and individuals that he's directly interacting with and discipling. In this case, the church planter is visiting prisons and is running a few feeding programs and afterschool Bible clubs.

This supervisor oversees nearly fifty centers or places where loving actions occur. Because these actions occur when he's not present, it creates a natural knowledge gap. He's close to the loving action, but he's not there. He doesn't know what's going on every day or even every week. In fact, it can be months before he gets a direct report.

Next, consider his supervisor. This area director has another fifty of these line supervisors who report to him. He may see them on average only twice a year. This system creates another serious distance between himself and his direct reports and the hundreds of preaching points in his area.

The area director also has a supervisor—a regional manager who has several area directors he oversees. They communicate by holding an annual meeting and through interagency correspondence; nonetheless, there's an even greater knowledge gap at this level.

Finally, there's a headquarters office with a president who oversees all the programmatic functions, training, recruiting, HR, administration, and fundraising. All these departments have their own interagency knowledge gaps as well. Above the president is a board that's even more removed from the ultimate loving actions of the ministry.

And this is an effective mission with a good rationale for its structure. But then, with the biggest knowledge gap of all, there's the investor who's focused solely on the loving actions of the mission and is perhaps somewhat suspicious of all these layers of management. (On this point, mission executives everywhere wrestle with the administrative overhead question in the perceived— and often real—issue that givers won't give above a specific percentage of their gift to administration.)

I've used a real-world example, familiar in all of its challenges, to illustrate the point. However, even a small start-up ministry will face its own knowledge gaps.

How do we solve this problem? Organizations try to manage their internal knowledge gaps by writing reports. Most programmatic people—in fact, most people I know—hate to write reports because they're nowhere near as much fun or satisfying as doing the work. Hence, reports are late, poorly written, exaggerated, extrapolated, condensed, ignored, or generally viewed like a visit to a dental office.

Yet they're important.

Organizations need to tell their stories, present statistics, and outline a coherent mission statement for their givers. This isn't an easy task; it's often done poorly, without adequately and accurately reflecting what's really going on—which is often marvelous and life-affirming.

Acquisition requires giving people a way in. It's good to remember: *the giver loves your purpose*. Your purpose is really all they need to care about. No matter the troubles you may have in delivering on your promise, it's what you care about as well.

Purpose begins with a statement, but it gains deep connection with the story that communicates the passion and struggle of your work.

Your Story

Most organizations don't give enough thought to this—or the right kind of thought. I can't tell you the number of training conferences we funded at First Fruit when I would get a report from the organization about an actual conference, and it was a series of quotes from participants that were left on their evaluation sheets. These usually noted that the conference was "incredible" or "life-changing," but with no depth of communication as to what was actually incredible or life-changing about it. Just a bunch of little bulleted statements of how this was an awesome experience, accompanied by a photograph of a bunch of people standing on a lawn or in front of a building.

If I hadn't personally attended some of those training sessions—something the vast majority of givers don't get to do—I would have been at a loss as to how to help my board understand the real value of what was going on. We even established a practice that each board member traveled every two years to close the gaps for themselves.

A well-crafted story can approximate being there if it's trustworthy and gives insights into the background and circumstances of the participants, perhaps told through the eyes of someone whose calling is impacted by the training.

Story is not about you or your organization, though either or both might be featured prominently in the narrative. Most importantly, it's not about sentimentality, which can be a trap, although it's a proven fundraising technique. Clearly, evocative images of a child with a distended belly triggers compassion in the viewer, and, with a few well-placed marketing phrases, can stimulate giving. You see the picture, and the loving action is assumed—the organization's purpose is right in front of your eyes. And if that doesn't seal the deal, there may be some trusted celebrity in the scene supplying an implied endorsement. On the surface, this appears to close the knowledge gap, but it's just sentimentality. That doesn't mean there isn't good work going on. But in my experience, it doesn't tell the whole story. It takes an incredibly sophisticated organization to help that child, something that's beyond the ability of most agencies to portray or compete with.

Tell your story, one that compels others to follow to the end. You need something of the craftsmanship of journalism. The storyteller may not be delivering the loving actions of the mission, but they're laboring to communicate who is doing what, where it's being done, when it's being done, and why and how. This journalistic "five Ws and an H" (Who, What, Where, Why, When and How) formula may be old, but it's a useful construct in serving good storytelling that connects with the listener. An organization helping hungry children can inspire us to understand how good can surmount evil.

STORIES PROVIDE DRAMATIC INSIGHT INTO THE INTERVENTION YOU'RE BRINGING AND HOW IT CHANGES THE "WHAT IS" TO "WHAT COULD BE."

A good and true story will take us into a situation that needs correcting—that is, the problem God is showing you. That story will provide dramatic insight into the intervention you're bringing and how it changes the "what is" to "what could be." It will tell the story of your mission by focusing on your actions and outcomes and will allow the process to be understood.

But here's the challenge. Who's going to write or produce these wonderful, life-affirming stories? Most organizations are too small and underfunded to have a staff position for a journalist. Additionally, most staff in well-functioning organizations already have more to do than time allows. There's also the question of talent.

Sometimes you just have to try doing it yourself. The best resource I know is *Go Tell It: How—and Why—to Report God's Stories in Words, Photos, and Videos,* a book by Jim Killam and Lincoln Brunner.[1] Both authors are practicing journalists who understand how to help most anyone get their story out.

If you have a Christian college nearby, it may have a communication department. In my experience, many of the talented senior students in this department are looking for good internships that offer real work to do and that can help them get a job. You can find Christians seeking internships at just about every secular university as well. Most ministries can offer a phenomenal opportunity to a talented, up-and-coming communicator because the ministry has such great stories to tell and can offer a student an opportunity to travel and perhaps even a small stipend. This minimal cost could provide your ministry a great return on investment.

White Papers

Let's look next at those three specific documents mentioned earlier as being particularly helpful in acquiring donors.

First, white papers help undergird your story. There's no one definition for a white paper and no single way to prepare one. In the context of your leadership and your organization, a white paper is an internal organizing document of no more than three to five pages. This paper handily sums up what your organization is about, what it does, what it has done, and what it wants to do. You'll use this document with your staff, board, key volunteers, and perhaps even a few donors to give them a glimpse into your work.

The white paper will be where you've prepared answers—well-written, concise, and dynamic—to those three big questions we discussed earlier for pinpointing a mission's purpose: What is God showing us, what is He telling us to do about what He's showing us, and how will we know we're accomplishing this calling?

Each of these questions should be answered in a half-page or less and be restated in a brief section when describing your vision and calling.

The way you answer these questions will demonstrate whether your organization is led by God or by men. This simple and small document is where you lay out how God has led in the organization's journey. Imagine a white paper being a representation of what you would say if you were walking along with someone and having a conversation about your work, helping the other person gain insight into what you do.

Additionally, your white paper should have brief sections about your organization's history, the passion behind why you do what you do, your values, your operating principles, your track record, your key and distinct strategies, and where you hope to take the organization in the future, as well as including endorsements from other leaders. In this list, don't pass over your passion element. This is a chance to help everyone know your innermost thoughts about your ministry. This is where you describe what animates you; what gets you up in the morning to go at it again; and what you'll do even if no one's funding you to do it.

From the giver's perspective, white papers help your investors understand why they should trust you. From your board members' perspective, as well as the perspective of your key volunteers and staff, this helps them understand what motivates you beyond the most obvious answers that can be derived from the needs your organization is addressing.

Lastly, a white paper must include a section where you state *your* definitions of key working phrases and local jargon. This point cannot be overstated. Miscommunication has caused relational problems throughout human history, and your organization isn't immune.

If you're a church-planting organization, picture defining what you mean by the word "church" and you'll get an idea of the necessity to be clear about what the word means. Is it a group of individuals under a tree listening to a story? I've actually encountered this definition in the past, and I thought it was okay, given the circumstances. Or perhaps you would define a church as a group of worshipers led by a paid pastor in its own building.

Perhaps yours is a ministry that works toward village transformation. But what do you mean by that? Define the types of villages you work in. Define what you mean by transformation. Don't take this effort lightly. This isn't a toss-off exercise designed to just create work; this is nothing less than a self-defining document.

I have a friend who, when writing his white paper, spent

six months defining what's meant by the Great Commission. Even he would admit that might have been a bit excessive, but he wanted to understand a phrase so overused that it had lost tangible meaning for him.

Another friend, the founder of a large ministry of village transformation, could say in a few brief sentences what he and his organization wanted to see happen in a village and how they would know it had indeed happened. He did this by defining what that village would look like ten years after the work had been inaugurated.

Your white paper is where these definitional issues are explained. Meanwhile, in all your written communication, look for key words you may think are self-evident, but which might not be.

From six different white papers I recently reviewed, I've drawn the following examples of phrases in need of definition:

- business as mission
- incarnational ministry
- we network and partner
- sustained pillars of prayer
- gatekeepers in the city
- make meaningful contributions to society
- spiritual growth classes
- we bring hope
- we seek to transform secular places
- effective world-changers

I actually like all these phrases and words. They represent the organizational aspirations of good people who are sacrificially bringing the gospel into some of the toughest places on earth. I'm sure that when you encountered most of these words and phrases, you were immediately able to attach meaning to them, as I did. But you and I may have misunderstood. When I explored each in depth with the white paper authors, I found I was generally off-base.

For example, I took "business as mission" to mean creative access strategies in countries that won't allow a missionary to work openly. Instead, it was an investment strategy to alleviate poverty through the creation of jobs in an open setting. Both are valid definitions, of course, but they represent vastly different missional approaches. The key here is to be clear.

An effective white paper will become a source document for other papers that may be needed—ones that are more nuanced and fleshed out, and which carry the necessary detail to become an operating manual or the like.

Additionally, each of the headings and sections from your paper can form the basis for the various pages of your website. There's hardly a potential donor, volunteer, or worker who won't look first at your website or other social media presentations to gain insights into whether he or she wants to go further with you. In your search for new funding, your white paper will prepare you to write your letters of inquiry and your funding proposal— both of which we'll look at next.

Letters of Inquiry (LOIs)

Today, many givers don't want to receive a full proposal. Perhaps they don't want to read something that extensive, or, more charitably, they may not want to put you through all the trouble of writing a full proposal for something they probably won't fund. In some cases, donors—especially those with a more institutional approach—may instead have an application process they want you to follow.

In these cases, letters of inquiry are a better tool. If they're well written, they give enough background for a grant-maker to get a feel for a particular strategy or program, without the need for a full proposal. As a grant-maker, I can even request several LOIs from an organization for various projects and go on a shopping trip of sorts. This is where LOIs shine. Multiple LOIs also accomplish the task of providing a fuller understanding of the scope of a mission's work.

In fact, I suggest that ministries annually produce a one-page document for each of their programs, projects, and strategies as well as for their administrative needs. These can be compiled into a book that can be shared with advocates, advisors, and board members. They can be posted on social media and web presences as well. A good one-pager with a personalized cover note can also serve as an LOI.

What should be included in these one-pagers and LOIs? A brief description (one to three paragraphs) of the project, its key components, its personnel, and its reason to exist, followed by a paragraph that shows how this project fits into the overall vision and purpose of the organization. An embedded video and/or an evocative photograph should also be included. Finally, a timeline, a budget summary, and a statement of how much has been or will be raised within the time frame should be included.

Converting a one-pager to an LOI means adding a more complete explanation of the need being addressed by the project, the expected outcomes, and how the project will be evaluated. A cover note personalizing the LOI should acknowledge previous gifts or communications with givers.

Proposals

Proposals are an exercise in organizing your thinking and your approach to the potential givers. Proposals don't raise money, despite what people think. (I could make a living running proposal-writing classes because of the deep-seated belief that proposals raise money.)

Most proposals stink, no matter how well written they are. Why? Because they're inadequate representations of what's really happening. They're only an outline, a mere projection of an idea.

In both of the foundations where I worked, I was fortunate to have an expense budget and could get on an airplane to visit ministries in person. I made these visits because I couldn't make decisions based on the proposals I was reading; I had to get out there in the field to see what was happening.

For example, I was able to sit in a missions partnership meeting in a newly freed former communist nation where I listened for five hours as they figured out how to establish an elementary school. I learned about the struggle of missionaries and their need to take care of their families so they can do their missional work. Their pioneering work had already planted a nacient movement, and now they needed to build the infrastructure to see their newly planted churches to maturity. This helped me to understand why they were asking me to recommend a grant to help them take care of their families as opposed to an outreach grant.

From 1983 to 2009, I believe no one read more evangelical mission proposals than I. (This is a completely unsubstantiated fact.) Most days, my work was about money—or rather, talking about money.

Even today, I'm so immersed in the arcane details of money, you'd think it would get tiresome, but it doesn't, and here's why. This topic brings me every day into the presence of some of God's most precious saints, people who've dedicated their lives to bringing the good news of Jesus' triumph over death to the farthest reaches of the globe. These saints live in the truth that God is their inheritance, yet they need money for their work. And we need to give it, not out of compulsion, but out of the sheer joy of knowing the One who has given us life.

My long history of being a proposal reader and grant-maker has afforded me the benefit of seeing patterns. This, combined with the experience of innumerable site visits, helped me develop the ability to see through the written words to the reality that undergirded them. This wasn't easy, since most proposals are inarticulate representations of what's really going on in the field and how the money needed will actually go to work. Nonetheless, mission leaders, their boards, and even their fundraising experts labor under the belief that good proposals are the single most critical key to successful fundraising. In reality, before the proposal has even been read, most of the fundraising has already been accomplished (or has failed).

Proposals help bring completion to your fundraising efforts. Internally, a proposal can serve as your key organizational tool—a single place where you define your purposes and strategies. Externally, proposals are most effective when they serve as a visualization tool.

Proposal Effectiveness

When I say "most proposals stink," this isn't the expression of a jaded American foundation program officer. What I'm expressing here doesn't come from my reading of a few thousand proposals, but out of my travels to see in practice the furthest extension of the loving actions of mission organizations. I've had the privilege of witnessing the reality of those loving actions described in proposals and to observe the disconnect between the written words and their actual practice.

This disconnect is never completely eliminated, even in the most professionally written proposals. This fact helped me to place less weight on an organization's proposal and more weight on doing the hard work of seeing past them.

At First Fruit we often found ourselves working with overseas organizations that had never before received an American foundation grant. This meant organizations we worked with were often writing their first proposals, which led me to help these organization's leaders craft their proposals. In a fellowship of communion, once I decided to recommend an organization, I simply became a volunteer at the table.

More about Proposals and LOIs

A proposal differs significantly from an LOI in both length and content. During my time as executive director at First Fruit, as well as when I was general manager at Fieldstead and Company, my principals preferred proposals to be presented in three to five pages with enough information from which a decision could be made. They also wanted it in the voice of the organization, rather than being so professionally polished that it lost sense of the passion and people who were making the request. Three to five pages doesn't give you much room to unpack a complicated strategy or program, so I allowed for unlimited addenda (charts, romance language, stories, testimonials, board member descriptions, references, citations, etc.) that could be reviewed by the principals while making the decision.

Although the foundations where I worked preferred shorter rather than longer proposals, others prefer longer ones. (This is especially true of governments and their agencies.)

If you have experience in fundraising, you've realized that one proposal size doesn't fit all, so fundraisers must be adaptable. This is even truer when fundraising in a local setting that doesn't have a well-developed tradition of philanthropy. I've encountered new fundraising efforts in Asian, African, Middle Eastern, and Latin American settings where all fundraising is done orally and is based entirely on personal relationship and trust.

Earlier I told the story about helping the Christ for the City mission in Costa Rica catch the vision for obtaining local funding instead of relying primarily on North American resources. They were quickly able to obtain full funding from within Costa Rica for their annual budget, but there was nothing written in the way of a proposal. Everything was done with a handshake and in a communion of trust and accountability.

Additionally, business at that time was conducted exclusively in cash. The mission leader made an appointment with a businessman and sent a courier on a scooter to his office, where the donor went to his wall safe, pulled out a wad of local currency, gave it to the courier, and in turn received a handwritten paper receipt. There were no tax deductions, no official forms, nor any of the red tape associated with American grant-making. The "proposal" was oral—but complete in its own way. It told the mission's story, purpose, and budget. It gave a context for the giver to do his part and made the promise of follow-up reporting. Also, it invited further personal involvement. The gifts were based on long-standing trust and a compelling vision for involvement.

Some years earlier, I was introducing a national leader to a local businessman in California who I was just getting to know. The national leader and I planned to make a funding request at the end of the meeting and had no expectation that we would be getting any kind of initial response from the businessman. Instead, halfway through the meeting, the man got up and went to a corner of his office, called his wife, came back, sat down with his checkbook, and gave the ministry the largest single contribution it had ever received, by a long shot. And there was no written proposal.

IT'S YOUR PASSION MATCHED TO THE GIVER'S PASSION THAT UNLOCKS THE RESOURCES.

Just when you think you have it figured out, you don't. In the end, it's your passion matched to the giver's passion that unlocks the resources. But written proposals will help you be organized for the eventualities.

Approaching Your Proposal

There's no sure-fire formula for creating the best written proposal, but the things we looked at earlier as elements of excellence should form a proposal's basic outline: character, track record, purpose, strategy (the idea), plus the attitude and approach of pursuing a communion of giving and receiving.

Writing a proposal can be a daunting task because of expectations, so let's reduce the pressure. Write your first draft as if you're writing a letter to your favorite aunt, someone who loves you but isn't intimate with the details of what you do. Tell her what you're hoping to accomplish, what your obstacles are, and what's needed to overcome those obstacles. Tell her about your opportunities. Tell her about where you feel stumped and where you clearly know the way forward. Tell her a story that dramatically illustrates why you keep doing your work when everything's stacked against you. This is what's at the root of the passion that drives you.

For example, help your givers understand these questions: Why did you go to med school? Why did you decide to give up the lucrative medical career to work in the poorest neighborhoods? Why do you work for a handful of vegetables and a couple of eggs some tearful and grateful mother gives you for saving her child? Why are you motivated to bring the healing that Jesus promised into the darkest corners of our shared existence?

I haven't met anyone, truly called of God, who doesn't have a story to tell.

Further Proposal Guidelines

Finally, here's a list of things to do and not do in a proposal. (Though again, I want to emphasize that generally givers will let you know how they want a proposal prepared.)

1. Come straight out with your request at the start. Everyone knows what this is about—so get right to it. Avoid soft leads that begin with a sob story you hope will lead me to understand why you and I together are the solution to this problem. This approach makes the mistake of saying you have to hook me first to reel me in. The hook is already in if I'm reading the proposal.

Also avoid writing an epic poem—a proposal that describes the start of your journey, when your calling was a murky thought, then takes me all the way through your life until this moment of requesting funds so the hero can triumph over evil and live happily ever after. No—tell me straight out what you're asking me to do.

Personally, I like to see an offer (commonly known as the "ask"; more on this later) in the first paragraph. Anyone reading this proposal will know that it's going to be about money. So, at the top, after a few brief words of personalization and greeting, summarize your purpose and offer in a direct but courteous style that is culturally appropriate in your setting.

2. Avoid arm waving. Have you ever had someone who's so excited about what they want to tell you that they're waving their arms frantically? In a proposal, arm waving means you're making unsupported propositions and attempting to generate excitement, without proof it's warranted.

I read a proposal saying that the organization it represents believes that if we fund their request, we'll be helping to start a movement that will go global and make the world a better place to live. To make this happen, all we have to do is help them pay for a part-time office assistant and a couple of conference scholarships. It sounds overhyped, doesn't it? The thing is, we like this ministry and believe it can be effective. The problem is that the leader, attempting to communicate excitement, has overblown the proposal without editing it effectively.

The leader could have simply said the ministry wants additional funds for much-needed staff and for scholarships for the neediest delegates to attend their conferences, helping them make a significant step forward in the work they've been called to do. We want to support this mission because it's one of the only groups we know that can actually make a difference; but it's hard to get past the arm waving.

Remember, a proposal isn't going to raise the money for you—it's just a tool. Scour it for statements and assertions that might confuse your reader, or worse, set up an argument between you and the giver. Don't leave an unsupported assertion out there, or state something as fact that can be assailed by someone looking for a reason to say no.

Which leads to the next point:

3. Be the expert, but don't make statements that can't be supported. When God gives you a task and shows you the need He's called you to, in time you should become an expert on that particular need. In your proposal, you should be able to explain not only the larger picture (the overall ministry and circumstances you've been called to) but also the specifics that will be addressed by the particular program or strategy that needs funding.

But don't make assertions you don't back up. More often

than not, those things will doom your proposal. If the giver reacts to some statement in your proposal by thinking, "Yeah, right," or "I don't think so," your grant will be dead in the water.

If you state that homelessness is a growing epidemic in your community, make sure you back it up with facts, not just anecdotes. For example, to make the point that there are more veterans of the Middle East wars on our streets than ever before, I might be tempted to say, "Why, just yesterday, while walking in the alley behind the Rescue Mission, I encountered three men, huddled against a dumpster, hungry and desperate—all of whom had served in Iraq—and I couldn't help them because our beds were full." That statement may be evocative, but it's not necessarily an accurate depiction of the larger situation—unless I add that according to a research study by a local university and the Community Foundation of Orange County, more than 17 percent of post-9/11 veterans have been homeless for at least thirty days in Orange County. I then add, "We can make a difference with your help, and here's how."

In your setting, however, you may not be able to access research or statistics like this; nonetheless, do your best to be clear and substantive in your description of the need you're addressing. It is this kind of information that builds confidence in your donors. If the need seems compelling enough, perhaps based on your track record of figuring out past challenges, givers will trust you and donate.

Givers want to be able to trust you, whether statistics are available or not. Good and true stories can do the trick. The more you help them understand the nature of the problem you're addressing, the more they'll see their part and will be motivated to give to your mutual purpose and calling.

Although knowing what God has shown you is the first and most important question of fulfilling your calling, understanding what direction He wants you to head doesn't preclude further researching of the relevant issues to verify what you're instinctively moving toward. The key here is messaging—communicating what you're focused on and how you'll deal with it, no matter how large or small the problem may seem in general public awareness.

International Bible translation organizations like Wycliffe Bible Translators want all people to be able to encounter the word of God in their heart language, no matter the size of the people group. As a result, they put as much hard work into small populations as larger ones, because God cares about the individual and the nation. If you're called by God to meet a need, He'll give you the tools and resources required to accomplish it—no matter the size of your team or project. So, don't be afraid of the truth. Instead, be afraid of lying or even simply exaggerating. False claims may bring you money to do what you want, but at the potential cost of your soul.

One of the most sobering Scripture passages for anyone who purports to be doing God's work is this one:

> Not everyone who says to me, "Lord, Lord," will enter the kingdom of heaven, but only the one who does the will of my Father who is in heaven. Many will say to me on that day, "Lord, Lord, did we not prophesy in your name and in your name drive out demons and in your name perform many miracles?" Then I will tell them plainly, "I never knew you. Away from me, you evildoers!" (Matt. 7:21–23)

4. When it comes to describing your calling—the purpose and the destination of your ministry—remember not to put strategies here. Bringing up your strategies could limit your ability to communicate context. Clearly lay out your vision, beginning with a strong purpose statement. Draw from your white paper the required proposal elements for the project or program you're seeking funds for.

Budgets and Offers

The question, "How much should I ask for?" trips up just about anyone who's ever submitted a proposal. First, your summary budget tells a story, so be careful with it. I always looked at summary budgets and their details because they informed me about the priorities of the ministries seeking funds. I wanted to learn what their leaders found important. Good budgets don't lie. Your budget and offer tells the answer to this.

Again, the specific request should be placed at the beginning of your proposal. Although this request is commonly called the "ask," I prefer the word *offer*. As a concept, it more accurately describes what's happening. You're offering the person or organization an opportunity to join you on all or part of the journey to your purpose. You can call this "asking," but remember that your investors need you as much as you need them.

You could be asking for five dollars, fifty, five hundred, or fifty thousand—it's all basically the same. An offer should always be appropriate to the capacity and desire of the giver. This is important to understand, because it's hardly ever inappropriate to ask for too much—and almost always wrong to ask for too little.

There's no exact science for determining what's appropriate

to ask. Just let your offer be organic to your budget and needs. Your givers will train you in what's appropriate just by their responses to you—and before God, you'll want them to follow Paul's guidelines in 2 Corinthians 9:7: "Each of you should give what you have decided in your heart to give, not reluctantly or under compulsion, for God loves a cheerful giver."

When money goes on mission

Acquisition is connecting givers and receivers through their joint pursuit of the loving actions of the Gospel that the gift, or the money on mission, will support.

NURTURING

Sustaining a
Giving and Receiving Partnership

WE NOW LOOK at the task that has the greatest potential for creating a communion of giving and receiving.

Not long ago I was asked to speak to a group of givers gathered at a weekend retreat hosted by the Chalmers Center,[1] a seminal ministry dealing with understanding poverty's true causes and the best solutions for alleviation. The organizers wanted me to focus on the pitfalls of making gifts across cultures. I was told, "This is something you've talked about hundreds of times; it'll be easy." In that moment, I have to admit I agreed—and the trap was laid. I hardly prepared, thinking I had the topic wired.

But as the hour approached, a new thought seized my heart and churned my gut: *I need a fresh approach.* It came out of the blue, and I couldn't shake it off. This is not a good thought to have in a hotel room on the afternoon of your presentation, with your notes outlined and your tried and true PowerPoint dusted off. That's when you're supposed to be rehearsing your new snappy anecdotes, not scrapping your speech for something else.

Fortunately, in my ensuing panic, I reverted to prayer. As I prayed, I began to remember the dynamic simplicity of following

Jesus. I'd been thinking a lot about it lately—about how tech-
niques and practices I'd adopted had taken the place of a simple
relationship and could this be made simpler? But how should
that logic be applied to the complexity and nuanced world of
international philanthropy?

The answer slipped into my mind gently. *Focus on love.*

LOVE'S POWER

Before beginning my presentation, host Brian Fikkert, at my
request, read 1 Corinthians 13. I asked the participants not to
listen as if they were at a wedding, but instead to hear the words
as an admonition when making (or seeking) a gift.

Let's do the same here:

> If I speak in the tongues of men or of angels, but do not have
> love, I am only a resounding gong or a clanging cymbal.
> If I have the gift of prophecy and can fathom all myster-
> ies and all knowledge, and if I have a faith that can move
> mountains, but do not have love, I am nothing. If I give all I
> possess to the poor and give over my body to hardship that
> I may boast, but do not have love, I gain nothing. (13:1–3)

I once had a friend who'd helped launch several enduring
and impactful ministries. I asked him how he did this.

"If you want to look smart," he answered, "hang out where
the Holy Spirit is."

I find that statement both curiously vexing and comforting.
God isn't like my GPS commanding me to make a right turn. I find

it's often difficult to tell the difference between a good idea and an idea from God. As I discussed earlier, quite often they're not the same. This is always a challenge in cross-cultural grant-making.

In the above verses, Paul introduces us to how powerful love can be. His words are like the opening notes in Beethoven's Fifth Symphony. The words are jarringly powerful fusillades that demand our attention. What is this love that negates the smartest thoughts about the deepest mysteries and brings them to nothing in its absence?

He answers this question in the next few lines:

> Love is patient, love is kind. It does not envy, it does not boast, it is not proud. It does not dishonor others, it is not self-seeking, it is not easily angered, it keeps no record of wrongs. Love does not delight in evil but rejoices with the truth. It always protects, always trusts, always hopes, always perseveres. (1 Cor. 13:4–7)

This is at the heart of what struck me that day in my panic: *Have I brought these attributes to my work?*

Love is *patient*. This isn't a characteristic often associated with evangelical philanthropy on either the giving or the asking side. For that matter, patience is a rare attribute anywhere today. I know I struggle with delayed gratification and taking the long view of things. On the other hand, deadlines impose a necessary discipline in the life of a program. In giving, it's my experience that achieving balance is a worthy, but tricky, goal to achieve.

I'm reminded of Paul's use of the word *truth* here, especially as it relates to love and giving. There's nothing that can get

THE GIFT SHOULD BE VIEWED AS THE RESULT OF PARTNERSHIP BUILT ON TRANSPARENCY, WITH UNITY THAT STRIVES FOR TRANSFORMATION AND HONORS THE COMMUNION OF GIVING AND RECEIVING.

muddied quicker than the truth when it comes to the transactional nature of giving and receiving. We use the word *gift*, but in truth, we often view the money as flowing into a contracted situation in which results are promised. The balancing act here is to view the gift as the result of a true partnership built on transparency, with unity that strives for a true transformation and honors the communion of giving and receiving. As mentioned earlier, this fellowship is the key thing that the Lausanne Standards seek to engender. Trust and a mutual accountability are the foundational concepts of a real communion between givers and receivers.

It's in this state that our best work occurs. I find I strive for my best in an atmosphere of trust, protection, hope, and perseverance—essentially, all the love definitions Paul denotes for us. When I sense I'm loved and trusted, I do my best not to break that trust. In turn, I become something upon which the one who grants trust can rely.

This principle translates into grant-making that nurtures results and leaves no room for skepticism—the great corrupter of love. That's not to say that skepticism doesn't have a proper place in grant-making. In truth, good questions should lead to healthy discovery. Love needs to know those things in which to believe.

Love never fails. But where there are prophecies, they will cease; where there are tongues, they will be stilled; where there is knowledge, it will pass away. For we know in part and we prophesy in part, but when completeness comes, what is in part disappears. When I was a child, I talked like a child, I thought like a child, I reasoned like a child. When I became a man, I put the ways of childhood behind me. For now we see only a reflection as in a mirror; then we shall see face to face. Now I know in part; then I shall know fully, even as I am fully known. (1 Cor. 13:8–12)

My prayer is to hear more clearly from God—to know where the Holy Spirit wants me to do my work. In other words, to distinguish God's ideas from the merely good ones. Someday we *will* see clearly. For now, we need to let love guide our way. "And now these three remain: faith, hope and love. But the greatest of these is love" (1 Cor. 13:13).

The work of nurturing the giver must begin here, with this understanding clearly in mind.

A Pastoring Function

Writing later to this same church in Corinth, Paul expressed the following:

And here is my judgment about what is best for you in this matter. Last year you were the first not only to give but also to have the desire to do so. Now finish the work, so that your eager willingness to do it may be matched by your completion of it, according to your means. For if the willingness is there, the gift is acceptable according to what one has, not according to what one does not have. (2 Cor. 8:10–12)

Paul was pastoring his flock here. He was encouraging the Greek believers to follow through on their previous promises. But he was also saying, "Give as you can and wish." Right here is the principle for the third part of funding: *nurturing* the donor to the fullness they've chosen to express. In this light, fundraising is a pastoring function.

As investors are acquired, they enter the ministry's orbit as friends. At this point, they may not have any idea what they'll do next.

Think of your own giving history. Sometimes you plan to make only a one-time gift, perhaps to help a missionary with a one-time medical need or because you saw the Middle East refugee crisis on TV and felt compelled to do something immediately. Or perhaps you became intrigued by a presentation you heard at church, and you made a small gift, thinking, "Let's see how this goes."

Thoughts like these are common to the giving experience. The hard work of nurturing donors is the task of giving them further opportunities to move from the acquaintance level of the orbit to the friend level—and even closer in, if they choose. If they want to make only one gift, you won't know that unless you ask them again. If you're doing it by mail, you can't assume they're reading your offers—they probably aren't. It's a short distance from the mailbox to the trashcan for most of us. But maybe, the acquaintance will pause and read your letter and make another gift.

That's why you should be in contact with your potential givers on a regular basis. The fear of bothering your established givers may actually lead them to think you don't respect them enough to let them know what's actually happening in your organization, or, even worse, may lead them to forget you altogether. Give your donors a clear opportunity to hear from you. If after a couple of years they haven't responded, that may be your clue that theirs was a one-time gift. Your investors will talk to you through their actions.

If your givers are making larger gifts and you're having face-to-face meetings with them, you'll be able to get direct feedback. But even with a smaller donor—let's say, someone helped your mission buy a goat for a destitute family for a hundred dollars—you really don't know at this point whether he might be able to buy five goats unless you give him a chance. If someone can give you a $500 donation, is it possible he or she can give $1,000? All you have to do is to give your donors the opportunity to give again.

THE FEAR OF FUNDRAISING—RATHER THAN A LACK OF GENEROSITY—CAN BE THE SIGNIFICANT CAUSE OF MISSIONAL FINANCIAL SHORTFALLS.

Often, the fear of fundraising—rather than a lack of generosity—can be the significant cause of missional financial shortfalls. Those who live and work among the poorest people of the bottom billions on this earth know that their poverty doesn't prevent them from being generous.

Your work in these matters is the godly task of bringing everyone into your orbit to the fullness of their giving before God, no matter what the ministry's financials say each month. The work of nurturing is a systematic way of helping people move in and through your orbit.

Most people whom God has called to support your work will land at the friendship ring of the orbit and stay there while making the occasional gift, reading your materials, or watching your videos and praying for you. This is by far the most powerful engine of God's work around the world, whether it's the Mizo homemaker with her daily offering of a handful of rice or the wealthiest philanthropist puzzling over what to do next. I've met the Mizo homemaker—and I've served philanthropists. The homemaker and the philanthropists are more similar than different. They're *with* you. They're praying. They're supporting you. And this is good. This is when love morphs into something transformative and unlocks the loving actions of the gospel to occur.

Bernie May, a former president of Wycliffe Bible Translators, told stories that helped make Scripture come alive for me. When Bernie started out with Wycliffe, he flew planes for the mission, among other locales, in the Peruvian rainforest. One of the most impactful stories he told me took place in an isolated village. The cultural imperative of that people group dictated that when a man died, his widow was thrown off a cliff to the river below. The couple's belongings were then distributed among the remaining families. This village was the setting for one of the translation projects Wycliffe does so well: translating the gospel into the heart language of often small and faraway people groups.

In one such place was a missionary who was methodically translating the New Testament with the help of the village's chief. Aware of their treatment of widows, the missionary—on the very day villagers were preparing this terrible fate for a widow—decided to translate a portion of Scripture from James 1: "Religion that God our Father accepts as pure and faultless is this: to look after orphans and widows in their distress" (v. 27).

When the chief, who had developed a respect for the word of God and a belief in Jesus, discovered that Scripture abhorred their practice, he jumped up, exclaiming, "We must stop this practice! God, our Father, says we are to look after widows." That day, he stopped the practice of killing widows, and he organized a schedule for the people in the village to share meals and provisions with the woman whose life was spared that day. In time, the entire village came to Christ.

I was reminded of this story while talking with Kehinde Ojo of International Fellowship of Evangelical Students (IFES) when he told me about his home church, The Family Worship Center, in Abuja, the capital city of Nigeria. The church was founded twenty-five years ago by a young couple and has grown to several thousand members attending at various campuses. The church has an active missions and outreach program, *fully* supported by the congregation. Though located several thousand miles away from the Peruvian rainforest and with a vastly different culture, the word of God is just as alive in Abuja.

The ongoing violence in the northern reaches of Nigeria has had tragic consequences for the Christians living in that region, especially the Nigerian missionaries and pastors working from various denominations, many of whom have been martyred. But their widows are not without help. Family Worship Center is partially supporting more than 1,600 of these women with a monthly stipend drawn from designated donations averaging $40,000 per month. And they are continuing to send missionaries into the region with additional support from their congregational donations.

James 1:22 says, "Do not merely listen to the word, and so deceive yourselves. Do what it says." From the crowded and teeming capital city of Abuja and from a remote village in the Peruvian rainforest, we couldn't have two more perfect examples of what James meant.

In both of these stories, we find the transformative underpinnings of offerings, sacrifice, and faithfulness in the face of extremely difficult life circumstances. These loving actions of the gospel are a few of the many threads sewn into the dress of the Bride of Christ, the Church, to be worn at the wedding supper of the Lamb. Won't it be something to sit in communion at the banquet table with these widows and all who are the bride of Christ, at this great feast!

Then I heard what sounded like a great multitude, like the roar of rushing waters and like loud peals of thunder, shouting:

"Hallelujah!
    For our Lord God Almighty reigns.
Let us rejoice and be glad
    and give him glory!

For the wedding of the Lamb has come,
   and his bride has made herself ready.
Fine linen, bright and clean,
   was given her to wear."

(Fine linen stands for the righteous acts of God's holy people.)

Then the angel said to me, "Write this: Blessed are those who are invited to the wedding supper of the Lamb!" And he added, "These are the true words of God." (Rev. 19:6–9)

"He who testifies to these things says, 'Yes, I am coming soon.' Amen. Come, Lord Jesus" (Rev. 22:20). On that day, we will all be in communion together. Hallelujah!

When money goes on mission

> . . . there is a communion of giving and receiving in a mutual transformative relationship that achieves a mutual purpose: the loving actions of the gospel.

ACKNOWLEDGMENTS

WITH DEEP GRATITUDE TO:

Jon Bonk, former director of the Overseas Mission Study Center (OMSC), and Dwight Baker, now also retired from leadership at OMSC: I began developing and teaching these materials at OMSC more than a decade ago, beginning in the mid-90s. Jon, you have no idea how impactful our annual lunches were on my development in understanding Missions and Money, (also, of course, the title of your seminal book). Dwight, your counsel over the years about writing a book bolstered my confidence to try this.

Tim Halls, OC International, and Greg Pritchard, President of the European Leadership Forum: Both of you attended my earliest seminars at OMSC on these materials and helped through the years in clarifying the message herein and how to teach and write about it.

Brad Smith, President of Bakke Graduate University, who brought together a distinguished cohort of missionaries, majority world leaders, and scholars to spend an intense weekend with me, helping beat the key concepts of this book into something they would find helpful. Cohort participants included: Celestine Misekura, Alex Araujo, Sukhwant S. Bhatia, Roger Niemeier, Justin Narducci, Rob Brynjolfson, David Andrianoff, Sisay Desalegn, and Fekadu Shone.

Steve Johnson, Vice President of Phoenix Seminary; Gary Hoag, International Director, Evangelical Council for Financial

Accountability; Brian O'Connell, React Services; Fred Smith, President of The Gathering; and Tom Courtney, businessman and board member of the Lighthouse Christian Home: Your reading of an early draft helped in developing a coherent approach to the book and got me far more focused than I otherwise would have been.

Sealy Yates, First Fruit's book agent and my long-time friend: You demystified the whole process for me and deeply encouraged me every step of the way; and to Thomas Womack, Sealy's structural editor, who first began giving shape to my initial draft—forgive me, Thomas, for not, at first, seeing what you saw in the book.

Duane Sherman and Amanda Cleary Eastep, Moody Publishers: Duane, I pray this book rewards you for taking a chance on a 75-year-old rookie author. Amanda, I don't know anyone (except the next two people I thank) who made me work harder for a much better result, even though sometimes during editing it felt like I was the lunch entrée in the tiger compound at the Seattle Zoo.

Peter Ochs, Chairman of the Board of First Fruit, and Dr. Henry Cloud, author and member of First Fruit's board: I'm not sure how to thank you both since the assignment to write this book came out of a back-room conspiracy you two cooked up. Henry, it is a wonder you had any hair left after the two-day retreat you undertook to get me focused on how to be an author. And Peter, I want to make a joke here so that I don't get sappy, but I can't. Your constant cheerleading and encouragement got me through more hard days than I ever imagined would be part of forming these thoughts into something useful to the many ministries you and Gail have encouraged over the years.

Bev, my wife and collaborator of 35 years: How do I thank you appropriately for all the work that you put into making this a much better book? It's hard for me to know where I leave off and you begin. Amanda, who, more than anyone else could, saw your work up close, told me that right after I thanked Jesus for getting me through this, I needed to thank you. That seems inadequate, but it's all I've got—and, at least, it's in the right order.

My kids, Anne, Grace, Jeff, and Jessica: Annie, your thoughtful questions and insightful interest were strategic and timely; Gracie, your climb toward excellence, in the framework of the aspect of the gospel you were named after, inspired me through this project. Jeff, my brilliant son-in-law, the honest way you lead your life is a gift that inspired me to hold to the truth as best I could as I wrote; and, Jess, who brings calm and order to me with just a touch, life was so much better with you around while I was laboring on this project.

My dear father in the Lord, Rev. Lewis Whitehead: I know you are somewhere around the throne. If you get wind of this, this book and the life it represents would not have happened had you not seen something in me that I didn't know was there.

And, lastly, for all of you who knew you were mentoring me, and for those of you whose writing, preaching, and very lives inspired me, even though you never knew it but see a semblance of your thinking in the ideas contained herein, you might be right. I am, after all, a born imitator. If I got it right, I hope it brought a smile; if I didn't, shake your head, it won't be the first time I caused that reaction in you.

NOTES

Chapter 1: The Communion of Giving and Receiving

1. Daniel Watts, Every Generation Ministries; first ministry leader I coached, First Fruit Institute, 2010.
2. Henri Nouwen, *A Spirituality of Fundraising* (Nashville, TN: Upper Room Books, 2011), 52.
3. Dwight Gibson, former US Director of World Evangelical Alliance, face-to-face conversation, Newport Beach, California, 2003.
4. Brian Stiller, *From Jerusalem to Timbuktu: A World Tour of the Spread of Christianity* (Downers Grove, IL: InterVarsity Press, 2018), 2.
5. "Christianity in its Global Context, 1970–2020: Society, Religion, and Mission," Center for the study of Global Christianity, 7, June 2013, Gordon-Conwell Theological Seminary, https://www.gordonconwell.edu/ockenga/research/documents/ChristianityinitsGlobalContext.pdf.
6. Philip Jenkins, *The Next Christendom: The Coming of Global Christianity* (London: Oxford University Press, 2011), 1–3.
7. Roger Steer, *J Hudson Taylor, A Man in Christ* (Wheaton, IL: Harold Shaw Publishers, 1993), 316.

Chapter 2: Living Stones: The Foundation of Sustained Interdependence

1. Steve Corbett & Brian Fikkert, *When Helping Hurts* (Chicago: Moody Publishers, 2009).
2. A dialogue between Brian Fikkert of the Chalmers Center and Rob Martin of the First Fruit Institute, facilitated by Brad Smith of the Bakke Graduate University, "When Helping Hurts—When Money Helps" (Christian Leadership Alliance, Member Online Magazine, Spring 2018).
3. Statistics presented by Todd Johnson, Director of the Center for the Study of Global Christianity at Gordon-Conwell Theological Seminary (Lausanne Resource Mobilization Working Group meeting, Atlanta, 2007).

Chapter 3: Trust and Accountability: Fruitful Giving and Receiving at the Foot of the Cross

1. Alexander Chow, "The Remarkable Story of China's 'Bible Women,'" *Christianity Today*, March 16, 2018, https://www.christianitytoday.com/history/2018/march/christian-china-bible-women.html.
2. ECFA.org, "ECFA History," http://www.ecfa.org/content/generalbackground.
3. The Lausanne Standards are a set of guidelines that lead givers and receivers through a simple process to achieve a true communion of giving and receiving.
4. "The Lausanne Standards," http://www.lausanne.org/content/the-lausanne-standards.

Chapter 5: Faith: Relying on God for His Provision

1. Roger Parrott, *The Longview: Lasting Strategies for Rising Leaders* (Colorado Springs, CO: David C. Cook, 2009).

Chapter 6: Excellence That Leads to Effective Giving and Receiving

1. Quote heard by Rob Martin at a presentation given in person by John Stott of Corinthians 8 & 9 entitled "Ten Principles of Christian Giving" at The Gathering in San Diego, CA, 1998.
2. John Stott, *The Grace of Giving, Money and the Gospel* (Peabody, MA: Hendrickson Publishers Marketing, LLC, 2004).

Chapter 12: The Orbit: The Accountability Effect on Giving and Receiving

1. One good way to understand this concept is to study what's known in organizational leadership as "S-curves." Two good books—*The Age of Paradox* by Charles Handy and *Jumping the S-Curve* by Paul Nunes and Tim Breene—have helped me.
2. Roger Parrott outlines this process in his book *The Longview: Lasting Strategies for Rising Leaders* (Colorado Springs, CO: David C. Cook, 2009), 141–51. Something I heard him say sticks in my mind: "I often get asked: How do I know we're providing a quality Christian education here at Belhaven University? I have only a less than satisfactory answer: Come back to the fifty-year reunion of this graduating class and ask each person how their four years here impacted them as followers of Christ in their jobs and marriages. Otherwise, we just do the best we can every year." That's taking the long view while implementing tight short-term planning and evaluations.

Chapter 13: Discovery: Finding Those Who May Join Your Work

1. ECFA, www.ecfa.org.

Chapter 14: Acquisition: Communicating to Raise and Give Money

1. Jim Killam and Lincoln Brunner, *Go Tell It: How and Why to Report God's Stories in Words, Photos, and Videos* (Chicago: Moody Publishers, 2014).

Chapter 15: Nurturing: Sustaining a Giving and Receiving Partnership

1. Chalmers Center, https://chalmers.org.

GOOD INTENTIONS ARE NOT ENOUGH.

Keep exploring how you and your church can foster lasting transformation in the lives of the materially poor.

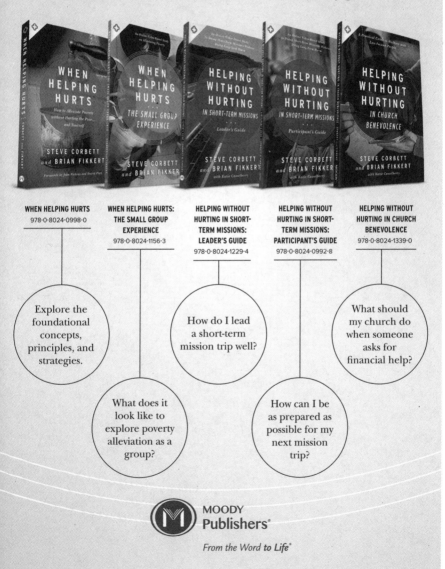

WHEN HELPING HURTS	WHEN HELPING HURTS: THE SMALL GROUP EXPERIENCE	HELPING WITHOUT HURTING IN SHORT-TERM MISSIONS: LEADER'S GUIDE	HELPING WITHOUT HURTING IN SHORT-TERM MISSIONS: PARTICIPANT'S GUIDE	HELPING WITHOUT HURTING IN CHURCH BENEVOLENCE
978-0-8024-0998-0	978-0-8024-1156-3	978-0-8024-1229-4	978-0-8024-0992-8	978-0-8024-1339-0

Explore the foundational concepts, principles, and strategies.

What does it look like to explore poverty alleviation as a group?

How do I lead a short-term mission trip well?

How can I be as prepared as possible for my next mission trip?

What should my church do when someone asks for financial help?

MOODY Publishers®

From the Word to Life®